# The Theory of Knowledge
# of Giambattista Vico

# The Theory of Knowledge
# of Giambattista Vico

by

Richard Manson

Archon Books
1969

SBN: 208  00899  3
Library of Congress Catalog Card Number: 71–96728
Printed in the United States of America

# Contents

# Acknowledgments

I want to thank the following authors and publishers for permission to quote from their works: Charles Edwyn Vaughan, *Studies in the History of Political Philosophy before and after Rousseau*, edited by A. G. Little, (Manchester University Press: 1925) New York: Russell & Russell, 1960; Henry Packwood Adams, *The Life and Writing of Giambattista Vico*, London: George Allen & Unwin Ltd., 1935; Robin George Collingwood, *The Idea of History*, Oxford: The Clarendon Press, 1946; Benedetto Croce, *The Philosophy of Giambattista Vico*, translated by R. G. Collingwood, (The Macmillan Company: 1913) London: George Allen & Unwin Ltd., 1915, New York: Russell & Russell, 1964; Arthur Child, *Making and Knowing in Hobbes, Vico and Dewey*, Berkeley: University of California Publications in Philosophy, 16 (1953): Thomas Berry, *The Historical Theory of Giambattista Vico*, Washington: The Catholic University of America Press, 1949; Giambattista Vico, *The Autobiography of Giambattista Vico*, translated by Max Harold Fisch and Thomas Goddard Bergin, Ithaca: Cornell University Press, 1944; Giambattista Vico, *The New Science of Giambattista Vico*, translated by Max Harold Fisch and Thomas Goddard Bergin, Ithaca: Cornell University Press, 1968; Robert Fling, *Vico*, Edinburgh: Wm. Blackwood & Sons, 1884; Karl Lowith, *Meaning in History*, Chicago: University of Chicago Press, 1949.

# Foreword

It is not enough and has never been enough to be an influential thinker and to pave the way for other influential thinkers. Vico certainly was, and a long list,[1] in which such diverse writers as Croce, Collingwood, Joyce, and Piaget are represented, can be found after his name. Plato and Aristotle were more influential and with good reason. But it is doubtful whether many men today, or even yesterday, could call themselves Platonists or Aristotelians and maintain that pose in the face of controversy. There is no doubt, however, that any man *realizing* Vico's dictum—that truth and fact are convertible—would call himself a Vichian,[2] and not only be able to maintain that position in the face of controversy, but meet with no controversy.

There have been few philosophers, especially epistemologists, who could honestly refer to themselves by the name of the schools to which they gave rise: that is to say, they did not act out their lives in conjunction with the principles they enunciated. In the West this criticism is

1. Giambattista Vico, *Autobiography*, tr. Max Harold Fisch and Thomas Goddard Bergin, 1944. See the introduction. Piaget is not included here, but might very well be.
2. The term is applied to periods rather than people. Its usage indicates, as Vico would say, that the idea does not require it of the language, i.e., there are no followers of Vico. This restriction is indicative of the lay as well as professional ignorance with which Vico is surrounded.

ignored. In fact it is never even levelled, apparently preferring to regard philosophy as mere mental gymnastics
having little bearing on life. But philosophy, when it is
not mere exercise, is supposed to have the greatest bearing on life.

This is where Vico stands out among epistemologists,
and this is why the present treatise is an exegesis on his
method: because in Vico theory and practice are one, and
because anyone realizing Vico's theory can put it into practice.

If philosophy is not mere erudition, if it is more than
ornament, it is something to be accepted or rejected
rather than displayed. A system of philosophy, a part of a
system, or an idea, to be accepted must meet a twofold
condition. First, it must *fit* the person considering it. This
does not mean simply that he must agree with it, but that
it must be agreeable to him, which is more than *liking*:
it must *fit* his whole personality, the way of thinking
and living he has chosen. Perhaps the reason there are so
many self-styled existentialists and phenomenologists today is because, assuming their sincerity, these systems or
their parts *fit* them. Secondly, a system must find support
in human experience. The reason existentialism or phe-
nomenology, as examples, exist at all is because their
systematizers have merely expounded what they experience in the human condition, or that part of the human
condition which these systems fit. The acceptance of a system of philosophy has a psychological basis and therefore
also an arbitrary one. But such acceptance also lends itself to a kind of Vichian interpretation, which renders it
less arbitrary: a philosophy that fits, or more likely a part
of one, is merely one that we are ready to accept at our
stage of mental development. It is one that we have already
devised ourselves, although unconsciously. This is why it

fits into our own unrealized system. We have created it unconsciously, but with the realization of *fit* we bring it to consciousness. Systems of thought are the finished products for which the groundwork was prepared by human experience or a certain representative section of human experience. We are not limited to the particular philosophies of our age. A person can be a Vichian, for example, if the thought fits; it fits if to some extent it has been created by him and can be incorporated by him. A person can also be a Vichian because Vico was and he is a member of mankind, and because what went into the composition of Vico's thought was prepared by mankind. Because Vico created a certain system that fit Vico, he can create all or a part of that system insofar as it fits him, and insofar as it fits him he has created it. Acceptance, however, has no bearing on truth, though the reverse may be the case. For truth we must look to Vico. Truth aside, what fits is accepted. What does not fit is rejected. But Vico's thought was and is part of human experience, and it will remain part of human experience as long as that thought continues to fit and grow with it.

Certain objections, which might prevent Vico's thought from being accepted as fully as it deserves, all of them minor, half of them false, and the other half concerning understandable matters, have been raised. For one, he was accused of using the very geometrical method he rails against. This is absurd. It can only be due to a superficial reading or an overlong look at his presentation or choice of terms. Secondly, Croce[3] alleged that Vico was inconsistent in his use of the words philosophy and philology. But Croce misread Vico on another score,[4] and one would

3. Benedetto Croce, *The Philosophy of Giambattista Vico*, tr. R. G. Collingwood, 1913, p. 34.
4. Karl Lowith, *Meaning in History*, 1949, p. 126.

be hard put to find anyone more consistent than Vico. A more valid objection, but one less related to his theory of knowledge, concerns Vico's patterning of the nations on the development of Greece and Rome. Actually, he found the law, pattern, model, or ideal eternal history exemplified *in* Greece and Rome, and was not completely unwarranted in concluding that the obscure periods of other nations also followed this pattern.[5] It is unfortunate that Vico did not have more facts concerning more nations at his disposal. He was an expert in Greek and Roman history on the one hand, and on the other he was in no position, as today, to consider adequately the histories of other countries. Secondly, Vico used Greece and Rome to fulfill his criterion of *nation*. Although there were other *countries* that did not conform to the ideal pattern Greece and Rome did, they were not entitled to be called *nations*. Their failure to so conform therefore did not matter. Such is the vice of attempting system.

The final objection concerns Vico's reliance on providence—as the indirect force behind man's making of history, the source of the ideal eternal history; as the guarantor of the method of introspection—and on divine knowledge as the measure of human knowledge. Both this and the preceding point objected to are consequences of the time in which Vico lived. That he was a good Christian and a devout Catholic and lived in an age when religion and God had to be considered need not discourage us from accepting the truth of what he says. Nor does this detract from the truth he found. Providence was important to Vico, but it need not be important to us. We can get along

5. C. E. Vaughan, *Studies in the History of Political Philosophy, Before and After Rousseau*, v. 1, 1925, p. 226.

in his theory and make use of it quite well without it. For the indirect force of history we can backtrack one step to the ideal eternal history, or simply the law of history; the method of introspection can be guaranteed but one step removed from God by the common consciousness of the race on the principle of the uniformity of human nature; for the measure of human knowledge the ideal of knowledge can be substituted. To do this would still be to do justice to Vico, but it would not be completely Vico. It would still be systematic, but it would not be his complete system.

For some reason philosophy has required system. This is where philosophers get bogged down, in pushing the truths they have gleaned to what seems to be their only logical conclusion and forcing them to turn around on themselves. This is also why philosophy which is not systematic is looked askance at in the schools. The theory of knowledge of Giambattista Vico is beautifully systematic. But it was pushed to what in our time could be considered an unlikely extreme. Vico would ask that we consder his system in the light of his time, but that we consider his truth in the light of all time.

# 1

## Introduction

## The Influences for
## Vico's Theory of Knowledge

Vico's theory of knowledge takes its start from both a refutation and acceptance of certain ideas of knowledge, of history, and of historical knowledge which his immediate and more distant predecessors held. As a point of departure we may therefore trace by Vico's own hand, using his own genetic method, the influences both positive and negative for the development of his theory, the resulting theory of knowledge itself, and the method and results of its application. To this it may be objected that the author of a work is never a sound judge of what was necessary for its composition. But when the author is also the originator of the principle that history cannot be more certain than when the one who creates it also narrates it, the objection in this case may be overlooked.

A reader of any of Vico's works must be instantly impressed with the overwhelming passion he had to unite, once and for all, the hitherto separate fields of philosophy and philology.* Indeed, the authors he extolled

*By philology Vico means the study of the effects of history as contained in languages and things, while philosophy is the study of the

were (the philosopher) Plato and (the philologian) Tacitus, whose points of view he attempted to synthesize within
himself, as his *New Science* is an attempt at a synthesis of
these two forms of knowledge. Vico regarded Tacitus as the
exemplar of practical wisdom, who knew man as he is,
while the universal knowledge of Plato disclosed man as
he should be. His admiration for these two men led him
to see the necessary unity of practical and intellectual wisdom, of fact and idea, or the 'is' and the 'ought'. By his
own account[1] it was this admiration which foreshadowed
his plan for an ideal eternal history traversed by the universal history of all times, in conformity to which the particular histories of nations developed, declined, and fell.

Vico was first led to seek this ideal eternal history in
Plato's *Republic*, but found the human mind too small
and the will too imperfect to devise a state approximating
it. Plato's *Republic* was an abstraction, any resemblance
to which could never be realized in the world of men.
The ideal eternal history could not be the idea of an abstract and immutable city or nation which all other cities
or nations exemplify. It had to be the idea of an order
which all nations follow in their particular histories. Plato's doctrine of forms, of succession, of modes of altera-

---

causes of history, as contained in ideas. While philosophy deals with
the world of ideas, philology is the study of the world of facts, com-
prising not only history, but music, art, science, politics, language,
and so on, considered as effects. It is the study of every factual aspect
of human endeavor, erroneously conceived in antithesis to philosophy, but in reality its handmaiden. Thus, anyone who studies the
facts of mankind, or of a section of mankind, Vico calls a philologian, for example Tacitus. A more complete explanation of this part
of the theory is given in Chapter V.

1. Vico, *Autobiography*, pp. 138–139. Vico refers to himself here
in the third person. He also uses the first person plural.

tion and corruption of governments was too narrow for Vico.[2]

On the other hand, Vico found that Plato's eternal idea, as the principle of all things, was established on the basis of the human mind's knowledge of itself. Certain eternal truths exist in the human mind but are not made by it. They must therefore be made by something superior to mind which is both independent of body and of time. This is the eternal idea which creates all things, and by creating them contains them within itself, thereby also sustaining them. Other truths are made freely by the human mind and contained within it. But unlike the former they are made in time, are dependent on the body, and since they are not founded on the principle of the eternal idea have less reality than truths which are eternal.[3]

These external truths, at the head of which Vico placed the ideal eternal history, according to him Plato rightly conceived to be contained in the divine mind. He refers to Plato's God as pure mind, in which all causes are contained. The ultimate reality is, therefore, mind. And since God endowed the human mind with these eternal truths, man's insight into his own mind, an image of the divine mind, is the means to understanding the world. According to Vico, Plato's tripartite universe comprises: the metaphysical world of God, who alone can know it because he alone created it; the mental world of man who can have knowledge of it because he made it; and the physical world of man, who can have certainty of it but not knowledge, because he did not create it.[4]

2. Robert Flint, *Vico*, 1884, p. 179.
3. Vico, *Autobiography*, p. 127.
4. H. P. Adams, *The Life and Writings of Giambattista Vico*, 1935, pp. 210, 211.

Vico held that the course or pattern the nations follow is ordered by divine providence. This pattern is an eternal truth and as such is contained in the eternal idea. Plato's eternal truths are therefore what Vico calls his *authority* for the ideal eternal history. In other words, Vico has found confirmation for his thought in Plato. He finds further confirmation and elaboration, i.e., *authorization*, in St. Augustine. Augustine, he writes, formed the idea of an "indirect and immanent" providence which works through nature and secondary causes to secure the progress of all of human society, while at the same time permitting individual freedom.[5] Vico asserted that Augustine had an idea of providence very similar to his own, where the particular interests and desires of men were made means to serve the wider ends of divine reason. The point at which they diverge, however, is where Augustine concerns himself no longer with the ordered development of human nature and its institutions, but with eschatology, redemption, and predestination.[6]

It is concerning the idea of providence that Vico disavows other of his predecessors. Since providence is responsible for the course the nations take, neither chance (Epicurus, Hobbes, Machiavelli), nor fate (Zeno, Spinoza) has any place in the scheme of things. On the contrary, the facts show that it is providence that directs human institutions, for which Vico cites Plato and Augustine as his authorities. He goes on to write that Cicero's idea of providence is likewise correct, while Pufendorf rejects it altogether, Selden assumes it, and Grotius ignores it.[7]

5. Vico, *Autobiography*, p. 44.
6. Flint, p. 180.
7. Giambattista Vico, *The New Science*, tr. Max Harold Fisch and Thomas Goddard Bergin, 1961, p. 383: 1109.

These last three, Grotius, Selden, and Pufendorf, Vico takes to task on other counts as well, never tiring of raising their names in connection with the principles they failed to enunciate. He writes, for example, that having taken little or no account of providence these philosophers were of necessity incapable of understanding the natural law of the gentes, since that law depends on the actualization by providence of man's potentiality for good as based on human freedom and sociability. For the same reason they also failed to distinguish between the natural law as it applies to the gentile nations, to the Hebrews, and to the philosophers. While the gentiles discovered the natural law by means of the ordinary action of providence, the Hebrews were helped both by ordinary providence and the direct intercourse of God. The natural law of the philosophers, on the other hand, was developed by reason and not through custom, and their concept was formed 2000 years after the nations had effected theirs.[8] Due to this confusion on the part of the 'natural law theorists' they believed natural equity to have existed and been understood by the nations as they understood it from the very first. According to Vico, it actually required 2000 years for the philosophers to develop the concept.[9] Grotius, Selden, and Pufendorf also erred, he writes, by beginning their histories with nations already developed and related to one another much as they are today. On the contrary, though, the original nations consisted of no greater units than families.[10]

8. Ibid., pp. 48–49; 310, 311, 313.
9. Ibid., p. 51: 329. This objection falls under the category of the Conceit of Scholars, one of Vico's rules of historical criticism.
10. Ibid., pp. 49–50; 318.

Despite the errors of Grotius, however, he found a stimulus in him for his ambition to reconcile philosophy and philology. In his work Vico saw how the knowledge of universals, philosophy, and the study of particular facts, or philology, could be combined to constitute one form of knowledge.[11]

Vico writes that from Hobbes he received great confirmation for his idea that civil philosophy was demonstrable. Reading Lucretius and others, he was led to find the true beginnings of civilization not, as was held, in wisdom, but in animal instinct appropriate to the first men. Lucretius also showed him how speech originated in gestures and how writing[12] first took shape in hieroglyphs, the two of which he was later to establish as beginning and developing simultaneously. Here he was also influenced by the fourth and last author whom he resolved to never lose sight of, whose method he admired, and upon whose *Cogitata et Visa* he sought to model the *New Science*. He writes of himself that "now at length Vico's attention was drawn to Francis Bacon . . . He marveled that one sole man could see in the world of letters what studies remained to be discovered and developed, and how many and what kinds of defects must be corrected in those it already contained,"[13] returning again to the recurrent theme of which he never loses the thread, the union of philosophy and philology.

In all these writers Vico was able to find some confirmation for his thought, notwithstanding their deficiencies in one respect or another. These deficiencies he categor-

11. Vico, *Autobiography*, p. 155.
12. Ibid., p. 42.
13. Ibid., p. 139.

ized as the effects of dogmatism. Each of the writers Vico cites as having had some positive influence on his thought also served negatively as a constant reminder to him not to read his own principles into the history of humanity. From Plato to Grotius each used a method that was abstract and not concrete, and none attempted the union of ideas with facts, of philosophy with philology, which he deemed necessary for a complete understanding of history. Their concept of natural law, for example, is that of an abstract idea formed and understood by primitive men, which has remained unchanged and valid down to the present day. According to Vico, however, the idea of natural law can neither have been formed nor understood by the first men since the formation of any idea requires reason, and these were men of almost pure instinct. Secondly, he considers natural law not an immutable idea, but a mutable fact which differs for different nations at different times. The reason these philosophers went wrong is because they began their inquiries with their own abstract rationalizations, and this because they saw human history and its institutions as constant or fixed instead of evolutionary. They separate institutions which have evolved out of human nature and thus introduce abstract entities, or fictions, into history. Vico on the other hand sees human nature and history as a process joined from beginning to end, where each stage and every element in every stage is interrelated. He deals with man as he manifests himself in specific, concrete institutions such as the family, the state, and so on, while his predecessors see him as neither related nor real.[14] For these

14. Vaughan, pp. 209, 210, 211, 212, 214.

reasons the forms of knowledge which he calls philosophy and philology are actually inseparable, both as the method for dealing with history, and as the actual method by which human thought has developed.

The final author and the one who had the most profound negative influence on the thought of Giambattista Vico was René Descartes. Vico attacked Descartes on four distinct though related points. First of all, as a student of history, a teacher of rhetoric, and a master of poetry, language, and law, Vico abhorred the Cartesian philosophy which excluded history from among the sciences and denied that it could be known. History and related matters were for Descartes based on tradition and authority and therefore sense-experience which, since it does not admit of certainty, cannot yield knowledge. Certainty could only be achieved by means of clear and distinct ideas, from which mathematical ideas could be postulated and the entire physical world reconstructed, of which there was then knowledge.[15] No wonder that under the impetus of Descartes the sciences of the physical universe flourished while history, considered a mere chronicle of incertitudes, became an ever more barren field.

For Vico, denying the possibility of history ever being more than a collection of verbal or written testimonies meant discounting that area in which man is most creative and therefore that area which is most knowable to him. He therefore criticized the Cartesians for not having "pressed forward the study of philology far enough for philosophers to see whether it could be reduced to philosophic principles."[16] Descartes abandoned history after he had shown that it rested on testimony and thus did not

15. Lowith, p. 118.
16. Vico, *Autobiography*, p. 38.

admit of true knowledge. What he failed to see was that history is not a matter of testimony. It is the inner world of human experience and as such could not be adequately dealt with by the Cartesian criterion of truth or knowledge as the clearness and distinctness of ideas. That criterion ignores the human factor creating and thus making knowable matters of non-sensuous experience. Vico rejected the rationalist abstractions of the Cartesians and set up instead, neither the senses nor the intellect, but the creative reason as the final determiner of historic truth.[17] Cretive reason is for Vico both the means by which the historian can have a true knowledge of history, and the means by which man has, in fact, made history. Human nature and its institutions cannot be deduced from abstract postulates. It can only be interpreted as it comes from experience. A static and changeless matter can be dealt with by analysis. But history, which is an ongoing process, can only be known by taking into account the processes of human reason and human progress, i.e., by the historical method.[18]

To save history from destruction at the hands of the Cartesians and traditionalists, who regarded it merely as a matter of conjecture, Vico decided to create a new science of history. This would depend on the creative human spirit and therefore involve everything obscure and contingent in human affairs, concerning itself with such subjects as "languages, poetry, eloquence, history, jurisprudence, politics."[19] The entire moral sphere was to be made knowable. In short, Vico sought to do for history what Bacon had done for nature, to establish principles of his-

17. Vaughan, pp. 239, 240.
18. Ibid., p. 252.
19. Vico, *Autobiography*, p. 38.

torical method along lines similar to those which Bacon had established for experimental.[20]

Opposed to the method of Descartes, which had proved so fruitful in the physical sciences, though not in the historical, and which began by rejecting all previous systems of thought,[21] Vico wanted to evolve a method which would revitalize history, and was to consist in the synthesis of all previous systems insofar as he held them to contain elements of truth. He considered the Cartesian method inapplicable to history, which is why Descartes failed to recognize the validity of historical knowledge. In history Descartes' problem, the problem of skepticism, is nonexistent. The question of the relation between ideas and the facts which they represent does not come up.[22] In an historical perspective the idea of an event and the event itself are one and the same. For this very reason, among others, the method for dealing with ideas and facts must be united in what Vico calls the combined philosophical-philological method.

Secondly, according to Vico Descartes' method of doubt fell short of its mark; for after having doubted all but the certainty of his own thinking and existing, he nevertheless failed to solve the problem of skepticism and, hence, to erect a science on the basis of that solution. Vico writes that "a skeptic will deny that the knowledge of being can be obtained from the consciousness of thinking. For to know, he insists, is to be acquainted with the causes from which things are produced; but I who think am mind and body, and if thought were the cause why I am it would be the cause of body, yet bodies are things

20. Vico, *The New Science*, p. 26: 163.
21. Adams, p. 208.
22. R. G. Collingwood, *The Idea of History*, 1946, p. 66.

which do not think. It is just because I consist of body and mind that I think, so that body and mind in union are the cause of thought; for if I were body alone I should not think, and if I were mind alone I should apprehend by pure intellection. That I think is not the cause but the sign of my being a mind, and a sign is not a cause. A skeptic of sense and discretion will not deny the certainty of signs, but he will deny the certainty of causes."[23]

Descartes had indeed proved that the certainty one has of one's own thinking and existing is indubitable. It is the certainty of consciousness, which no skeptic would doubt. It is not, however, a truth based on knowledge; not *scientia*, but only *conscientia*.[24] Knowledge is by causes, and since man knows neither how or why he thinks nor how or why he exists (since his thought does not cause his existence), he can have no knowledge at all, but only consciousness. And consciousness is not knowledge. If he had the causes, he would know, but since he does not have the causes he only thinks he knows. The clearness and distinctness of ideas is adequate as a criterion of consciousness but not of knowledge. Being merely subjective, it can yield only certitude, not truth. What is needed "is a principle by which to distinguish what can be known from what cannot; a doctrine of the necessary limits of human knowledge."[25]

This doctrine, which is Vico's answer to skepticism and the basis for his science of history, is that "the rule and criterion of truth is to have made it. Hence," writes Vico, "the clear and distinct idea of the mind not only cannot be the criterion of other truths, but it cannot be

23. Flint, p. 92, from Vico's *De Antiquissima Sapientia Italorum.*
24. Vico, *Autobiography*, p. 38.
25. Collingwood, p. 64.

the criterion of that of the mind itself; for while the mind apprehends itself, it does not make itself, and because it does not make itself, it is ignorant of the form or mode by which it apprehends itself."[26]

It would follow from this doctrine that since only God can be said to have made truth only he can be said to have knowledge of it. Since he has made all things he contains within himself the causes of all things and therefore knows all things. Science is knowledge by causes. Since man has not made the world he does not contain the causes of its being within himself. Therefore a science of the world is not accessible to him. The human condition would appear to be that of consciousness rather than knowledge, of certitude rather than truth, of *cogitare* instead of *intelligere*, or thought instead of understanding.

Since God's knowledge is by causes it is a demonstrative knowledge. Man, apparently limited to consciousness, can only observe. There is one science, however, of which man is capable, though it is not a science by causes but only of causes. The science of mathematics yields knowledge in the same way that God's knowledge is derived by demonstration—not, contrary to Descartes, by self-evidence.[27] Mathematical knowledge is possible because what the mathematician creates or constructs is out of elements contained within himself and therefore knowable to him. Unlike God's world, however, the world which the mathematician creates is a fiction based on abstractions—definitions, postulates, axioms. Consequently, though the knowledge derived by mathematics fulfills the requirements of knowledge, it is not a knowledge of reality but only of unreal and arbitrary constructions.

26. Vico, *Autobiography*, p. 38, from *De Antiquissima*.
27. Ibid., p. 39.

Furthermore, while mathematics taken by itself can yield knowledge, if only of fictions, when applied to other sciences the most it can yield is probability or certainty. According to Vico the geometrician demonstrates because he creates, but the physicist cannot demonstrate because he does not create.[28] Such sciences as physics remain indemonstrable for two reasons: first, because their subject-matters cannot be created and, second, because interpreted mathematically, they become fictive. Also, the definitions, postulates, and axioms with which mathematics deals are static and avail nothing to the physical sciences, where the elements are complex and constantly changing. Descartes was in error in applying the geometrical method to physics and other sciences. The only adequate method for dealing with the physical sciences is for Vico the experimental method of Bacon. A knowledge of the physical universe can only be had concerning those aspects which lend themselves to imitation.[29] Yet because the scientist does not create, but can only imitate, the world of nature, at best all he can do is approximate a knowledge of the physical universe which, because God has created it, only he can know. The scientist must be content with the certainty which comes from consciousness. The rule formulated by Vico to judge the value of any science is based on the distinction he draws between truth and certainty, as derived from knowledge and consciousness. Any science insofar as it contains more abstract or fictive elements is a science of the certain based on consciousness, while insofar as it contains more reality deals with truth as derived from knowledge. Physics is truer than mathematics because it contains more reality. Mathematics is more certain than physics because it contains more ab-

28. Ibid., p. 38, from *De Antiquissima.*
29. Ibid., p. 39, from *De Antiquissma.*

stractions. The historical sciences would appear to be truer than physics then but less certain.[30] Thus, by a criticism of Descartes Vico has relegated the sciences Descartes extolled to the same sphere as the historical sciences Descartes depreciated. None, it would seem, can give man knowledge. The human condition is apparently one of consciousness alone.

30. Ibid., from *De Antiquissima.*

# 2

# The Possibility of Knowledge and the Limits of Knowledge

As a Christian Vico believed in the absolute creative power of God, who because he creates all things contains the causes or elements of all things within himself and therefore knows all things. In order to ascertain whether or not human knowledge was possible Vico was led to inquire into the nature of divine knowledge, or knowledge itself, and to see if there was a similar faculty in man which approximated in any way that of the divine. To do this he enlisted the aid of philology considered philosophically. Inquiring into the *Ancient Wisdom of the Italians*,[1] Vico finds that they regarded truth as simply fact, or what is made. God as the first maker contains the first truth. As the maker of all things his truth is infinite. As he makes all things out of elements contained within himself his truth cannot admit of error. The ancient Italians regarded the divine mind as intelligent, since it contains and disposes all the elements of what it makes. The human mind, on the other hand, only possesses thought, since it is incapable of combining the elements of things. It can therefore think things but not intellectually comprehend, or know, them. The human mind is thus said to participate in reason but

1. Flint, pp. 86–88, from *De Antiquissma*.

not to possess it. Since knowledge or truth is what is made science is the knowledge of the form in which the mind, by composing the elements of a thing, makes it. Divine knowledge is whole, because the divine mind contains and therefore comprehends both the internal and external elements of things. Human knowledge is only of parts, because the human mind can only grasp the external conditions of things. Since the human mind cannot know the whole of things, but only their parts, it cannot attempt to add the parts together into a whole, but only to divide them into smaller parts. Only divine knowledge is comprehensive. Thus Vico describes human knowledge as a matter of division. Human science is like an "anatomy of the works of nature." Unable to grasp the whole of things, it has divided man into body and soul; it has subdivided the soul into intellect and will, and the body into figure and movement. From intellect and will it has formed being, and from figure and movement unity, and divided the sciences accordingly. Metaphysics thus becomes the science of being, arithmetic the science of the unit, geometry of figure, mechanics of external motion, physics of internal motion, medicine the science of the body, logic of the intellect, and moral science of the will. In short, unable to know the whole of things and thus to possess what might be called "the science of the whole," the human mind contents itself with knowing parts, and assigning a particular science to each part.

Since truth and fact, as derived from knowing and making, are identical, and since God is the absolute maker, he is the absolute knower. The divine mind, in making things, contains the causes of things within itself. And since truth consists in the causes of things, truth is contained within the divine mind. Knowing is an activity of the creative reason, which is not an attribute of God, but is that in which God consists. In God reason and being are identical, as knowing and making are likewise identical in him. He cannot know without creating, nor create without knowing. Thus, nothing is apart from God or alien to him, but everything is contained in and generated by the divine reason. God, therefore, or the divine reason, is the source of all truth, and is himself the first truth.

Since divine reason is a creative faculty God's knowledge is intuitive and immediate. It consists of the genera or forms by means of which a thing comes into being. Such knowledge is of the entire truth, which is the whole of reality. The human mind, on the other hand, proceeds by reasoning instead of intuition, and on the basis of abstract ideas instead of universal forms. It attempts to grasp reality through its parts, whereas a true knowledge of reality is only attainable as a whole.[2] The result of this attempt is what Vico calls the anatomy of science, where by dissecting its objects the mind diminishes them.

Should man's mind be capable of grasping the whole of reality, i.e., of comprehending the entire truth, that would be tantamount to either entering into, or becoming, the mind of God, which is impossible. It would seem, then, that a knowledge of reality can only be had piecemeal, which is not knowledge at all.

Unless it can be shown that there exists some area of human thought in which man can create reality and by creating it contain its causes within himself, thereby knowing it as a whole, then indeed the human condition is one of mere consciousness. In other words, unless there is some one area in which human reason resembles the activity of

2. Adams, p. 98.

divine reason in all areas, then a grasp of reality can only be piecemeal.

Vico holds that human science is the product of man's incapacity to grasp reality other than in parts, because it is external to him, and because he does not contain any of the elements composing the truth he is after. Since the criterion of divine truth is to have made it, human science will become certain to the extent that it can compensate for the incapacity of the human mind and simulate the creativeness of the divine mind, becoming akin to divine science.[3] Yet the physical sciences cannot give knowledge because the elements with which they deal are not created by the human mind and their causes not contained within it. The mathematical sciences, on the other hand, though the elements with which they deal are created by the mind, and their causes contained within it, cannot give a true knowledge of reality because they deal with only fictive entities. Although mathematics does deal with the whole, the whole with which it deals is not made of real parts, while the physical sciences proceed only by parts.

Because the human sciences are due to abstraction, Vico holds that the more they deal with corporeal matter the less certainty they have and the more truth. Mechanics is less certain than geometry and arithmetic because it deals with external motion. Physics is less certain than mechanics because it deals with internal motion. And morals is less certain than physics because, while physics deals with the internal motion of bodies, which is regular, morals is concerned with the motion of souls, full of vicissitudes and without limit.[4]

By an inquiry into the nature of divine knowledge Vico

3. Flint, pp. 89–90, from *De Antiquissima*.
4. Ibid., p. 90, from *De Antiquissima*.

has found the criterion of knowledge or truth. Inquiring into the nature of geometry he has found that human reason is a creative faculty resembling the divine. These investigations have also led him to conclude that the three elements, knowledge, will, and power, exist in the human as well as the divine mind.[5] Further, he has shown that in proportion as the sciences lose in certainty they gain in truth; and that the moral sciences, because they depend on the will, are the least certain.

> Now, as geometry, when it constructs the world of quantity out of its elements, or contemplates that world, is creating it for itself, just so does our Science (create for itself the world of nations), but with a reality greater by just so much as the institutions having to do with human affairs are more real than points, lines, surfaces, and figures are. And this very fact is an argument, O reader, that these proofs are of a kind divine and should give thee a divine pleasure, since in God knowledge and creation are one and the same thing.[6]

A true knowledge of reality is possible for the human mind insofar as truth can be created by the human mind. The limits of knowledge depend on the limits of the creative faculty of man. The area of human thought in which knowledge is possible and to which it is limited is the historical sciences, the moral sciences, or the new science, as created by Vico.

5. Vico, *Autobiography*, p. 156.
6. Vico, *The New Science*, p. 63: 349.

# 3

# The Criterion of
# Knowledge and Truth

Vico developed his criterion of knowledge, or of truth, on the basis of his understanding of the absolute creative power of divine reason, which is in possession of absolute knowledge, and on that of the procedure by which human reason operates in the mathematical sciences. In recognizing the failure of the Cartesian criterion of knowledge to refute skepticism, and thus to create an adequate theory of knowledge, he opposed it with his own original doctrine of knowledge. Accordingly in *De Antiquissima*[1] he states that the only way to overcome skepticism is to hold that the criterion of truth is to have made it. Skepticism, he says, rests on the contention that things appear to be different from what they really are, and that what they are in reality is unknowable. Skeptics do not deny cause and effect, though they do deny that the causes of things can be known, since the forms in accordance with which things are made are unknown. According to Vico, however, by the very admission of causes the skeptics refute their own argument, for the comprehension of causes contains all the forms by which effects are produced and is, therefore, the

1. Flint, pp. 106–107, from *De Antiquissima*.

first truth in which all things are contained. For the same reason it is infinite truth. Since body is only an effect it is prior to body, or spiritual, i.e., it is God. God, or the divine creative reason, is therefore the first truth, by means of which all human truth is to be measured. Skepticism is thus overcome by holding that the causes or elements of things are contained within the human mind and that, by coordinating them, they can be both made and known.

True to his method of joining philosophy to philology, and of pursuing truth with reason close upon the heels of fact, Vico finds authority for his criterion of knowledge in the ancient Italian language.[2] "To the Latins . . . ," he discovered, "*verum*, truth, and *factum*, fact, are reciprocated or, to speak with the vulgar of the schools, are converted . . . *Scire*, . . . to know, is to compose the elements of things . . . and in this way science is knowledge (*cognitio*) of the genus or of the mode by which a thing is made, knowledge by which the mind, while knowing the mode because it composes the elements, makes the thing." In short, "the mind cannot but make the truths that it knows." Thus, the necessary condition for a thing to be known is that it must be made; if it cannot be made, it cannot be known.

Knowing is synonymous with making, with composing the elements of things, i.e. with causing. Knowledge or science is, therefore, not of but by causes. Vico opposed Descartes' subjective certitude with Aristotle's definition of a science as that which one knows by containing its causes within oneself, by making it.[3] Hence, he insisted on verification instead of perception and self-evidence; on demonstration and experimentation instead of pure thought.

2. Arthur Child, *Making and Knowing in Hobbes, Vico, and Dewey*, 1953, pp. 283–284, from *De Antiquissima*.

3. Adams, p. 209.

By 'cause' Vico understood efficient cause in the widest sense as containing all the principles and conditions of causation by which existence can be adequately understood. 'To prove by causes', 'to collect the elements of a thing', 'to make' are equivalent terms for knowledge. Vico was led to seek "the congruity of effects with the causes assigned to them."[4] Such phrases as "Let that be granted which is not repugnant in nature and which we shall later find to be true in fact"[5] occur throughout his work. "If such an origin of cities (which later we find to be the fact) were offered as a hypothesis, it would command acceptance by its naturalness and simplicity and for the infinite number of civil effects which depend upon it as their proper cause."[6] "Such a constant and perpetual orderly succession of human civil institutions, within the strong chain of so many and such various causes and effects as we have observed in the course the nations run, should constrain our minds to receive the truth of these principles,"[7] and so on.

The cause of a thing is the whole explanation, reason, ground, or source of its existence, containing in it all the elements of the thing to be explained. To know is to ascertain the adequate cause of a thing, and since the only causes which can be ascertained are those which have been made, the criterion of knowledge is that it should be made. The only science or knowledge which deserves its name is therefore genetic. The first and foremost principle of the new genetic science of Vico is that "doctrines must take their beginnings from that of the matters of which they

4. Vico, *The New Science*, p. 335: 1020.
5. Ibid., p. 37, Axiom LXX: 248.
6. Ibid., p. 40: 264.
7. Ibid., p. 316: 980.

treat."[8] The method of the *New Science* is to "begin where its subject matter began . . . We must therefore go back with the philologians and fetch it from the stones of Deucalion and Pyrrha . . . With the philosophers we must fetch it from the frogs of Epicurus, from the cicadas of Hobbes . . . Our treatment of it must take its start from the time these creatures began to think humanly."[9]

In applying the principles of his new genetic science to the problem of the origin and development of the nations, Vico asserts that governments arise in accordance with the nature of the governed. Governments must therefore be interpreted in conformity to the nature of the governed. Laws, customs, and so on, must be interpreted in conjunction with the forms of government to which different human natures have given rise. Only in this way can the proper causes be ascertained and the facts which resulted from them be clearly and fully understood. Ignorant of these principles, Vico holds that scholars of Roman history were unable to relate the laws which were enacted at various times throughout the history of the empire to their proper causes in the forms of government which Rome instituted and ultimately in the natures of the people which gave rise to these forms. Thus, for example, the institutions which were actually effected during the form of government known as 'aristocratic' were mistakenly ascribed by the historians to the period they called 'popular.' By failing to establish the true historical method of finding the entire ground or cause for the existence of a thing, these historians failed to enunciate the foremost principle of the *New Science*, by which they would have seen that

8. Ibid., p. 49, Axiom CIV: 314.
9. Ibid., p. 57: 338.

nations, governments, laws are but customs developed naturally out of the nature of the people.[10]

Another principle of Vico's science is that "the nature of everything born or made betrays the crudeness of its origin." On the basis of this principle he established the origin of poetic wisdom.[11] Poetic wisdom, he wrote, was the first wisdom of mankind. Its first expression was that of theological poetry, which was naturally crude. As metaphysics is the first science, from which all the sciences arose, the beginning of poetic wisdom can be traced to a crude metaphysics[12] pertaining to the nature of the first men. Indeed, all the other sciences, from theology to politics, will be found to have been originally expressed in poetic form.

A final example of Vico's use of genetic method is his handling of the idea of natural law, which he holds was born when man first conceived the idea of divine providence.[13] For law originated when man began to restrain his bestial impulses, which could only have been due to the gradual awareness of a power greater than himself, namely, to an idea of deity.

The preceding remarks indicate that the criterion of knowledge and the method which results from it are perfectly fitted for application to the historical or moral sciences. Indeed, following Vico's definition of knowledge, history or morals is the only discipline which can truly be called a science. Since knowledge or science means to prove by causes, to collect the elements of things or, simply, to make, then history is eminently suited to being an object of knowledge; for, unlike physics, the world of history has

10. Ibid., pp. 301–302: 952.
11. Ibid., p. 69: 361.
12. Ibid., p. 72: 367.
13. Ibid., p. 84: 398.

truly been made by man and, unlike mathematics, it has been made out of whole and real cloth.

". . . in the night of thick darkness enveloping the earliest antiquity, so remote from ourselves, there shines the eternal and never failing light of a truth beyond all question: that the world of civil society has certainly been made by men, and that its principles are therefore to be found within the modifications of our own human mind. Whoever reflects on this cannot but marvel that the philosophers should have bent all their energies to the study of the world of nature, which, since God made it, He alone knows; and that they should have neglected the study of the world of nations, or civil world, which, since men had made it, men could come to know. This aberration was a consequence of that infirmity of the human mind by which, immersed and buried in the body, it naturally inclines to take notice of bodily things, and finds the effort to attend to itself too laborious; just as the bodily eye sees all objects outside itself but needs a mirror to see itself."[14]

In the world of history the human creative capacity is qualitatively identical with that of the divine and therefore human knowledge is qualitatively identical with divine knowledge. Here man is truly creative, for he contains the causes of his creation within himself. The cause of the historic or moral world is human nature, which requires nothing external to itself to produce its effect. From human nature customs arise, from customs laws, from laws governments, and the whole fabric of history is built-up from the one proper and efficient cause of human nature. A science of history as a science of what the human mind has wrought in the social world is therefore not only pos-

14. Ibid., pp. 52–53: 331.

sible but guaranteed. In addition, as science is a body
of knowledge the principles of which are eternal and immutable, then one may turn to God to find that man's
making of the civil world is done in accordance with
divine providence. The new science of history is thus both
a study of human nature and a rational civil theology of
divine providence. The principles on which the world
is founded are from God, but the actual founding of the
world is done by the free-will of the human spirit. Vico's
God acts "without the force of laws . . . , but making use
of the very customs of men (in the practice of which they
are as free of all force as in the expression of their own
nature . . . "[15]

Vico's deity established the nations through the 'vulgar'
wisdom of the human race, which is the common sense of
each people in agreement with every other. Human nature, in choosing to obey divine reason, fashions the world
of nations in accordance with this common wisdom of the
race, which determines the necessities and utilities common to all the nations, thus constituting the two sources
of the natural law of all the peoples.[16] Consisting of free-
will, the passions, and the necessities or utilities, man can
either act in conjunction with, or in opposition to, divine
providence. By controlling the passions, the human will
makes the world in agreement with the dictates of providence, which speaks through the common wisdom of the
people. By giving vent to the passions, necessities or utilities, the human will acts contrary to the immediate ends
of providence, but is still said to make the world in accordance with the immutable principles of wider ends.
Vico states that although men have, in fact, made the civil

15. Ibid., p. 382: 1107.
16. Ibid., p. 21: 141, 142.

world it has, nevertheless, originated in the mind of God, whose aims are always higher and occasionally contrary to the immediate ones men seek. Narrow human ends thus become the means to fostering the ultimate divine end of preserving the human race.[17] The institutions of religion and monogamy, for example, were established by men in order to avoid, respectively, fear and shame, while under the guidance of divine providence these institutions, including the custom of burial, were created for larger ends, viz., to serve as the primary foundations of society.

Notwithstanding that providence has been active in the making of the world of society, man may still be said to have truly made it. And because he has made it he contains the causes of its production within himself and can therefore know it. But the makers of society were not rational in their making, so that reason must evolve before the conversion to knowledge can take place. Knowing and making are convertible only when reason is present. Though the first men of the nations created the civil world, they created it out of their own corporeal imaginations. Their creation differed from that of the divine to the extent that imagination differs from intelligence. Whereas God "knows things and, by knowing them, creates them," the first men created things by imagining them, because of which they are called "poets," which is Greek for "creators,"[18] and because of which Vico describes the first wisdom of the race as poetic wisdom.

Because the world of society has been created by men in the past through imagination, it can be known by men in the present through reason, that is to say, through the fully developed creative reason which reconstructs the

17. Ibid., p. 382: 1108.
18. Ibid., p. 75: 376.

causes of man's first creations. The historian can know because he can recreate in his own experience the causes by which society has evolved. On the basis of the principle of continuity in human nature, the historian can verify in his own experience the experience of the first creators of the world. By looking into the modifications of his own human mind he can reproduce the natures of the makers of the customs, languages, laws, and governments of the world., i.e., he can compose, demonstrate, make, and therefore know the causes of history. "Indeed, we make bold to affirm that he who meditates this Science narrates to himself this ideal eternal history so far as he himself makes it for himself by that proof 'it had, has, and will have to be.' For the first indubitable principle posited above is that this world of nations has certainly been made by men, and its guise must therefore be found within the modifications of our own human mind. And history cannot be more certain than when he who creates the things also narrates them."[19]

19. Ibid., pp. 62–63: 349.

# 4

# The Method of Knowledge: Introspection, The Modifications of the Mind

The theory *verum et factum convertuntur* establishes that truth or knowledge is entirely the work of the mind, either the mind of God or of man. By knowing the causes one creates the fact, while by creating the fact one knows the causes. It follows then that there is no knowledge which exists independent of the mind which creates it. There is no fact which is purely objective, no truth which is absolute.[1] There is nothing arbitrary about truth or knowledge thus created since, according to Vico, all scientific truth, all the truths which are made, are eternal and immutable.[2] They are found in the divine reason, with which human reason, insofar as it creates the civil world, is qualitatively identical. Consequently, it is by means of introspection into the modifications of our own human mind that truth or knowledge is to be created.

The principle on which the validity of the method of introspection rests is that of the uniformity or continuity of human nature. As the world of history has been made

1. Flint, pp. 98–99.
2. Ibid., pp. 100–101, from *De Antiquissima*.

out of the modifications of the human mind in the past, so the world of history can be known by the modifications of the mind in the present, for human nature is essentially always and everywhere the same. The self-identity of humanity guarantees the method of looking into one's own mind in order to reconstruct and thereby know the mental states which have resulted in the institutions, languages, customs, laws, governments, of humanity. Behind the various expressions of the different aspects of human institutions there is a mental language common to all the nations which grasps what is uniform in human society. This is proved, for example, by proverbs in which, though expressed differently in different nations and at different times, the same meanings are conveyed. By virtue of this common mental language Vico believed his *New Science* would be able to construct a common mental vocabulary for all ancient and modern languages.[3] On the basis of the principle of the uniformity of human nature he thus arrived at a solution of the problem of the origin of languages. By showing that meanings were not determined by convention but arose naturally he established that they have natural significations. The reason there are many languages instead of one is because the natures of the various peoples have been altered by their environments. Different environments have given rise to different natures and therefore customs, which together have resulted in the formation of different languages. The fact that proverbs are semantically the same though they differ in their forms of expression confirms this for Vico.[4]

However nations may differ then they share a common mental language, a common nature, which derives

3. Vico, *The New Science*, p. 25, Axiom XXII: 161.
4. Ibid., pp. 104–105: 444–445.

from the essentially uniform nature of man. All nations must therefore pass through essentially the same development. The development of nations is identical with the development of the human mind. History is thus the science of the progressive unfolding of the human mind. The *New Science* is the "history of the ideas, the customs, and the deeds of mankind." From the ideas, customs, and deeds of men are derived the principles of the history of human nature, the same as the principles of universal history.[5]

In order to reconstruct the mental stages by which history developed, Vico had to begin his science, in accordance with his genetic method, where the matters which it treats begin, namely, at the dawn of human consciousness. To discover the nature of human institutions the *New Science* had to begin with an analysis of the first human thinking concerning the necessities and utilities of social life. The first men, the progenitors of mankind, evolved the proper form of human nature in its two aspects of body and mind.[6] The historian, or philosopher of history, can therefore look into his own mind, in its proper aspect as a product of history, to induce those original forms of mind by which history has been produced. By performing an introspective analysis of his own mind he can recreate the process of historical development[7] by which human nature and the institutions created by it have evolved. To do this he must uncover the way in which the first human thinking took shape. He must remove himself from the historical perspective in which he is and rethink the thoughts proper to such savage and wild natures

5. Ibid., p. 73: 368.
6. Ibid., p. 214: 692.
7. Thomas Berry, *The Historical Theory of Giambattista Vico,* 1949, p. 91.

as the first men must have had.[8] By the axiom that science must begin where its subject matter begins, the *New Science* must proceed from the time "the first men began to think humanly and," as Vico says, "not when the philosophers began to reflect on human ideas."[9]

Vico's predecessors failed by not beginning their histories genetically and therefore by attributing to the founders of society a faculty of reason as fully developed as their own. Instead of beginning with the external world, they should have begun with a history of human ideas, on which the metaphysics of the mind proceeds, since this history is internal to the mind of whoever meditates it. Because the world of nations is the result of mind, it is within the modifications of the mind that its principles will be found.[10]

Vico thus finds the key with which to unlock the nature of the first human beings and, simultaneously, the causes of human institutions. The principles of the origin of languages and letters which together comprise the whole of history, are found in the fact that the first men, in accordance with their nature, were poets and spoke in poetic characters. This is the master key of Vico's *New Science*, which required twenty years for him to discover.[11] It is because the forms of the human mind have become so refined that an inquiry into the original mental states of mankind, by means of introspection, is fraught with interminable difficulties. For the poetic wisdom of the first men began with an imaginative metaphysics, unlike the ra-

8. Vico, *The New Science*, pp. 57–58: 338.
9. Ibid., p. 62: 347.
10. Ibid., p. 74: 374.
11. Ibid., p. 5: 34.

tional and abstract metaphysics of the philosophers.[12] Ignorant of their poetic nature, and assuming a rational nature, previous philosophers of history failed to align the proper causes with their effects. Consequently, they could not descend into the imaginations of the first men, nor begin to reconstruct the process of universal history.[13] Vico, on the other hand, recognizing the validity of the method of introspection, and having discovered the master key of his science, was able to enter, through his own mind, the minds of the first men; there to ascertain the precise nature of their thinking, and by rethinking their thoughts, in the way they thought them, to recreate the process of history. Having found that the first men were instinctively poets,[14] that the world they inhabited therefore consisted of poetic nations,[15] and that all the necessities and utilities of life were created in the poetic centuries thousands of years before the arrival of the philosophers,[16] the question then became—what was the nature of these first men who were poets, creators, i.e., in what did their poetic wisdom consist? By means of analogies drawn from children, contemporary savages, and mutes, and by looking into his own mind, Vico discovered that "the first founders of humanity applied themselves to a sensory topics, by which they brought together those properties or qualities or relations of individuals and species which were, so to speak, concrete, and from these created their poetic genera."[17]

12. Ibid., p. 74: 375.
13. Ibid., p. 84: 399.
14. Ibid., p. 29: 187.
15. Ibid., p. 33: 216.
16. Ibid., p. 33: 217.
17. Ibid., p. 123: 495.

Vico found that human consciousness had dawned in the form of sensation, which is an active faculty, creating the world by means of impressions. Once consciousness is awake and sensation alive, memory comes into play by recalling past sensations. Imagination follows memory, creating images from it as from a storehouse. And intellect, though dormant, is also present. Memory occurs in these three primary operations of the mind: it is sensation in remembering impressions, imagination in changing and generalizing from them, and intellect or invention in putting them into proper perspective.[18] Between sensation and intellect lies imagination, which is the primary operation of the poetic form of the mind, that which characterizes the poetic nature of the first men. But since the first men relied more on their physical than their intellectual qualities, though sensation, imagination, and intellect pertain to the mind, they were exercised in terms of the body.[19] Sensation, imagination, and intellect are regulated by what Vico calls the Art of Topics, which is concerned with inventing or creating. The Art of Criticism, which is concerned with judging, necessarily developed later. Since the first men were poets—creators—sensation, imagination and intellect, but especially imagination, are the three primary operations of the mind by which they did their creating.

The Art of Criticism falls under the category of philosophy, occurring 2000 years after the category of poetry, which is the language of the imaginative faculty. Although human nature is always and everywhere essentially the same, and the modifications of the mind in which it manifests itself are the same, contrary to Descartes different

18. Ibid., p. 260: 819.
19. Ibid., p. 216: 699.

forms of the mind by which these modifications are devised predominate at different times depending on the progress of the historic cycle.[20] As children are more imaginative than rational, so in the childhood of the race man abounds in imagination rather than reason, in accordance with the axiom that to the extent that intellect is weak imagination is stronger.[21] The first men proceeded to create their world through the faculty of imagination rather than by pure or abstract thought. Incapable of forming intelligible universals they fashioned imaginative universals, by means of which, for example, the image 'father' signified his entire house. Unable to comprehend abstract forms they imagined corporeal forms, which they vivified by likening them to themselves.[22] Thus, for example, they created Hereditas to be the embodiment of hereditary property. Characteristic of this individualizing mentality is the inability to conceive of spirit as distinct from body, or of power or force as distinct from something manifesting it. Myth and fable are accordingly the natural vehicles through which the poetic nations expressed themselves. It is thus that Vico finds the origin of the poetic characters out of which fables are constructed. By certain axioms he establishes the natural *genius* of primitive men to think in terms of fables and myths. Since they were unable to create intelligible genera, they created poetic characters or imaginative genera, under which they subsumed all the particular species resembling them.[23]

Because all men at the dawn of human consciousness thought in terms of imaginative universals, and because

20. Croce, p. 45.
21. Vico, *The New Science*, p. 29, Axiom XXXVI: 185.
22. Ibid., p. 341: 1033; p. 342: 1035.
23. Ibid., p. 32: 209.

it is axiomatic that uniform ideas originating among alien peoples share a common ground of truth,[24] Vico contends that myth and fable, as products of the common wisdom of the peoples, are true forms of knowledge. Mythology is actual history, conceived by minds in which concepts are inseparable from the experience in which they occur, in which events cannot be conceived apart from the individuals associated with them. "Man in his ignorance makes himself the rule of the universe, for in the examples cited he has made of himself an entire world. So that, as rational metaphysics teaches that man becomes all things by understanding them (*homo intelligendo fit omnia*), this imaginative metaphysics shows that man becomes all things by *not* understanding them (*homo non intelligendo fit omnia*); and perhaps the latter proposition is truer than the former, for when man understands he extends his mind and takes in the things, but when he does not understand he makes the things out of himself and becomes them by transforming himself into them."[25] This is Vico's vindication of the non-logical or pre-philosophical forms of knowledge by which primitive minds must have proceeded. The myths and fables, the laws, languages, and poetry of the ancient peoples are vast repositories of truth, in error only as to their form of expression. At the time when men could only think in terms of individuals or imaginative universals their laws, for instance, were enacted only in response to some event which necessitated them, and then they only applied to that particular event.[26] Not until later, with the progress of the mind from sense to reason, when human consciousness became fully developed,

24. Ibid., p. 22, Axiom XIII: 144.
25. Ibid., p. 88: 405.
26. Ibid., pp. 125–126: 500.

did the laws become generalized, eventually to evolve into legal concepts of universal validity. By an inquiry into the modifications of our own human mind it can be shown that these first laws differ only in their form. They are what Vico refers to as truths under masks.[27]

Having looked into his own mind and in it found the forms of mind by which the first men must have created their world, Vico proceeded to reconstruct the thought which did the creating. For such thoughts are modifications of the mind of him who thinks them, in which are contained the origins of all the customs and institutions of the nations. Since man has made this world out of the modifications of his mind the historian can remake and thereby know it out of these same modifications. To reconstruct such thoughts as these first men must have had it was necessary for Vico to replace the predominantly rational form of his mind with their imaginative nature, yet at the same time to retain as much of his rational faculty as was necessary in order to grasp the causes of what he was thus reproducing.[28]

His procedure is first of all to discover what institutions the modifications of the human mind have given rise to which are common to all men. These he finds within the modifications of his own mind to be the customs of religion, marriage, and burial, which were instituted by all the nations and with which humanity began. Since he found these to be the universal and eternal customs of the nations, he made them the three primary principles of the *New Science*.[29]

Concerning the first of the primary modifications of the

27. Ibid., p. 343: 1038, 1036.
28. Cf. ibid., p. 76: 378.
29. Ibid., p. 53: 332–333.

human mind, in which the institution of religion has its origin, and because of which consciousness first appeared, Vico writes that since the first men were all passion and little reason it will be in the 'vulgar metaphysics' of the theological poets that the fearful idea of divinity will be found. Fear of this divinity caused man, through the exercise of free-will, to first restrain his passions, which act of self-consciousness is the beginning of consciousness, and then to transform them into more human ones, which is the beginning of humanity. In order to know how man first began to think humanly it is necessary to begin with the one notion that is proper to the earliest mentalities. "That notion we show to be this: that man, fallen into despair of all the succors of nature, desires something superior to save him . . . Confirmation (of this) may be found in a common human custom: that libertines grown old, feeling their natural forces fail, turn naturally to religion."[30]

As Vico proceeds to uncover the causes of the institutions of humanity by means of his method of introspection, he also shows how he is able to correct errors and misconceptions in history. He finds, for instance, that Roman history, as it was previously written, contradicts basic human nature. The historians held that the plebeian struggles first occurred over the issue of *connubium* because of the desire for nobility, second over the consulate because of the desire for honor, and then over the priesthood because of the desire for wealth.[31] But it was rather to gain wealth that the plebeians fought over and received certain ownership of the fields; then, in order to leave the fields intestate to their heirs they fought for the right to sol-

30. Ibid., p. 58: 340, 339.
31. Ibid., p. 320: 986–987.

emn matrimony, by which their children became legal. And finally, in acquiring these rights they immediately became full citizens. Vico reasoned that the common civil nature of men, which is found within the modifications of the human mind, shows that the order of human desires is to seek wealth first, then honor, and nobility only last.

To sum up, "the proper and continual proof here adduced will consist in comparing and reflecting whether our human mind, in the series of possibilities it is permitted to understand, and so far as it is permitted to do so, can conceive more or fewer or different causes than those from which issue the effects of this civil world. In doing this the reader will experience in his mortal body a divine pleasure as he contemplates in the divine ideas this world of nations in all the extent of its places, times, and varieties. And he will find that he has thereby proved to the Epicureans that their chance cannot wander foolishly about and everywhere find a way out, and to the Stoics that their eternal chain of causes, to which they will have it the world is chained, itself hangs upon the omnipotent, wise, and beneficent will of the best and greatest God."[32]

Mind is as much a product of history as history is a product of mind. The most original contribution which Vico passed on to history, philosophy, or the philosophy of history, is the thought that the outward manifestations of history can be found within the modifications of the human mind, and that the development of history can therefore be followed through the stages of the mind's development. The progress of history is determined by the progress of the mind, from its beginning in consciousness to its end in knowledge, from the first form in which it is found, that of sensation, through the intermediate form of im-

32. Ibid., p. 61: 345.

agination, to that of reason. History begins when mind begins, i.e. when man first becomes conscious of himself through sensation. Between the individualizing faculty of sensation and the universalizing faculty of reason lies imagination, through which man becomes conscious of a power greater than himself, viz. God, and becoming conscious of God, he later becomes conscious of other men. In other words, by means of the capacity allotted him for forming imaginative universals man's first thought grasps the first truth, the idea of deity. Though the form is in error the content is correct, so that consciousness is said to contain truth, however imperfect. And imagination is said to contain the seeds of reason, which as it develops perfects the truths first grasped by imaginative universals. Hence, Vico contends that poetry, the primary form of the mind, in which languages and laws, myths and fables find expression, contains truths formed by imaginative universals. For this reason the first men are to be considered the founders of the arts, whereas the philosophers, who came 2000 years later with the development of reason, founded the sciences, in this way completing humanity.[33]

As philosophy, or the language of reason, is said to consist of esoteric wisdom, so poetry, or the language of the imagination, is said to consist of vulgar wisdom. The *New Science* is thus a history of human ideas, displaying the origins both of the practical sciences of the past and of the speculative sciences of Vico's day.[34] This history of human ideas as contained in the wisdom of poetry is verified and complemented by the history of philosophy itself, for the first attempts at philosophy were made on evidence derived

33. Ibid., p. 124: 498.
34. Ibid., p. 82: 391.

from sensation.[35] Poetry, which is the natural vehicle through which primitive peoples express themselves, deals with the senses, as grasped by imaginative universals, while philosophy, concerned with reason, grasps rational universals. The truths which are contained in poetry are therefore identical in content with those derived by philosophy, though the former are imaginative in form while the latter are rational. "As much as the poets had first sensed in the way of vulgar wisdom, the philosophers later understood in the way of esoteric wisdom; so that the former may be said to have been the sense and the latter the intellect of the human race. What Artistotle said of the individual man is therefore true of the race in general: *Nihil est in intellectu quin prius fuerit in sensu.* That is, the human mind does not understand anything of which it has had no previous impression . . . from the senses. Now the mind uses the intellect when, from something it senses, it gathers something which does not fall under the senses; and this is the proper meaning of the Latin verb *intelligere.*"[36]

The mind is the mind's own work, insofar as it is the product of the stages through which it has passed. Sensation contains the seeds of imagination, which contains the seeds of reason. Were it otherwise, consciousness could never have evolved. For if the mind had not first sensed things, it could never have imagined them. If it could not imagine things, it would never have passed the stage of bare sensation; nor would reason have developed from and reformulated the truths of imagination. It is only through the intermediate stage of imagination that sense

35. Ibid., p. 124: 499.
36. Ibid., p. 70: 363.

and reason were gradually combined until reason became fully developed and truth perfected.

History is likewise the mind's own work, insofar as the customs and institutions of the nations have developed out of the modifications of the mind during these same stages. "That which did all this was mind, for men did it with intelligence; it was not fate, for they did it by choice; not chance, for the results of their always so acting are perpetually the same."[37] Barbaric customs and institutions developed from a lack of reason and unbridled passion, while the emergence of civilization was due to the development of reason and the restraint of passion. For this reason, although the customs and institutions of society are effects of the mind, they are not necessarily, and not at all in the obscurer times, effects of rational minds. Indeed, the more distant and obscure the period under consideration, the less does reason prevail, and the more is society revealed to be the work of the imaginative form of the mind. Yet truth is contained in the non-rational forms of mind, so that in order for the historian to study the obscurer periods it is necessary for him to enter into these forms. He will then find in the modifications of his mind the origins of the institutions, such as the ancient laws, languages, and especially poetry of the first men, developed under these forms. He can do this because the faculties by which they created these institutions contained the seeds of reason, because these institutions were created of and by the mind, and because human nature is a continuous development, at the end of which the historian, because he subsumes the forms through which humanity has thusfar passed, places himself.

The truths of history are therefore to be found in the

37. Ibid., p. 383: 1108.

various stages of the mind's development. Thus, the category of poetry as distinct from that of philosophy, and the idea of poetic or imaginative universals becoming rationalized into philosophic universals. The non-logical forms of knowledge by which the first men proceeded to construct their world are not only vindicated but exalted. These men constructed their world out of consciousness rather than knowledge, and on the basis of certainty rather than truth. Their creating depended on facts, rather than ideas, and on authority rather than reason. History is therefore a composite of ideas and of facts, of reason combined with authority, of the truths which come from knowledge united with the certainties of consciousness. Since knowledge or truth is fact, or what is made, to make truth the historian must make it in the way it was first made, i.e. by means of the vulgar wisdom of consciousness, while to know truth he must know it by the rational wisdom of knowledge. History cannot be known by reason alone because it was not made by reason alone. By the same token there can be no such thing as a rational philosophy of history. On the other hand, history cannot be known until the historical process itself has reached fruition in reason, when the historian can turn back, not reading reason into the development of humanity and its institutions, but reviving and reliving the imagination with which man fashioned himself and his world. The historian's knowledge must accordingly consist not merely of rational wisdom but of the vulgar wisdom of the first men as well. For this reason, the method of historical knowledge is well-suited to the particular subject matter to be known. It is the combined method of ideas and facts, reason and authority, truth and certainty, knowledge and consciousness; in short, philosophy-philology.

# 5

# The Method of Knowledge:
# Philosophy - Philology

Vico's criterion of knowledge sets the limits of knowledge or of truth to what is made. Anything which is unmade is unknown. Since knowledge and truth are one
and the same, there is no unmade and thereby unknown
truth. One's own existence is also unmade and therefore
cannot be known. Descartes' attempt to refute skepticism
and find a basis for knowledge in the doubtlessness of
one's own existence failed because individual existence is
unmade by man and thus unknowable by him. According
to Vico there is only consciousness of one's own existence,
though this consciousness is not open to doubt. The opposite of doubt is not truth, whose opposite is falsity, but
certainty. Individual existence is therefore a certainty.
The certainties of consciousness are unmade, undemon-
strable, and therefore unknown, but nevertheless perfectly
valid forms of thought. They are 'lesser' or undeveloped
truths to which the criterion of truth does not yet apply.[1]
The realm of certainty is composed of beliefs and persua-
sions, what Vico calls the facts of consciousness as opposed

1. Flint, p. 95.

to the ideas of knowledge. Since these certitudes are not founded on the basis of reason their validity is established on the authority of the common consciousness of the race. To the study of certainty Vico gives the name philology, whereas philosophy is the study of truth.

The distinction which Vico draws between knowledge and consciousness and truth and certainty is precisely that which he finds manifested in the history of human thought and its institutions. It is an axiom of his that "men at first feel without perceiving, then they perceive with a troubled and agitated spirit, finally they reflect with a clear mind. This axiom," he writes, "is the principle of poetic sentences, which are formed by feelings of passion and emotion, whereas philosophic sentences are formed by reflection and reasoning. The more the latter rise toward universals, the closer they approach the truth; the more the former descend to particulars, the more certain they become."[2]

Since the actual procedure for the evolution of human thought has been from consciousness to knowledge, from certainty to truth, and from authority to reason, the actual method used to understand the process of historical development is that which unites these terms under the general title of philology-philosophy. It is also axiomatic that "men who do not know what is true of things take care to hold fast to what is certain, so that, if they cannot satisfy their intellects by knowledge (*scienza*), their will at least may rest on consciousness (*conscienza*)."[3] Hence, "the true and the certain may be combined and harmonized, and the greatest of the sciences is that in which this is accomplished—the science which results from the concur-

2. Vico, *The New Science*, pp. 33–34, Axiom LIII: 218–219.
3. Ibid., p. 21, Axiom IX :137.

rent action of philosophy and philology. Philosophy and philology embrace the whole of man's intellectual acquisitions. Philosophy is the science of the absolute and immutable; philology, which includes literature and history, is certainty as to the relative and temporary. The former deals with the ideas which are the objects of reason; the latter with the facts which are produced by the human will. History is a rational process which begins with the certain separated from the true, and ends with the true united to the certain. It can be explained neither by a geometrical method on the one hand, nor an empirical on the other, but only by the cooperation of a philosophy which duly regards facts with a philology which duly regards ideas."[4]

By philology Vico means the study of the facts formed on the basis of authority, on which is founded the consciousness of what is certain in human affairs. By philosophy he means the study of the ideas formed by reason, from which is derived the knowledge of eternal and immutable truth.[5] The goal of philosophy is to recreate and thus understand the causes as contained in the ideas of history, while the goal of philology is to recreate and understand the effects as contained in the facts. However, the causes, or the ideas, of history have no reality except as exemplified in their effects, and the effects, the facts, of history cannot be understood apart from their causes. Consequently, an adequate knowledge of history can only be obtained by a method which grasps both the causes and the effects, or the ideas and facts, the truths and certainties of historic development.

4. Flint, pp. 97–98, from *De Antiquissima*.
5. Vico, *The New Science*, p. 21, Axiom X: 138.

Philosophy and philology had always been two separate disciplines, the one concerning the ideal, the other concerning the factual or real. While the latter dealt with facts, or the certainties of authority and could at best give only probable knowledge, the former dealt with absolute and immutable truth, having no foundation in reality. The philosophers went astray by not grounding their reason in the certainties of the philologians, while the philologians failed by not receiving sanction for their authority from the truths of philosophy.[6] Philosophy contemplates man as he should be, in idea; philology as he is, in fact.[7] In order to have a true science of human nature and its history the deficiencies of the ideal and the factual forms of knowledge must be compensated for, and they can be by uniting them under one method. The truths of philosophy must be verified in reality, that is to say, they must be made concrete, paying due respect to the individual facts of history. Philology, on the other hand, must be rewritten in terms of philosophical principles. This way the facts of history can become the objects of true knowledge. The certainties of philology will then be seen to have their basis in eternal truth. In his *Autobiography*[8] Vico writes that he "finally came to perceive that there was not yet in the world of letters a system so devised as to bring the best of philosophy, that of Plato made subordinate to the Christian faith, into harmony with a philology exhibiting scientific necessity in both its branches, that is in the two histories, that of languages and that of things; to give certainty to the history of languages by reference to the history of things; and to bring into ac-

6. Ibid., p. 21: 140.
7. Ibid., p. 20 Axiom, VI-VII: 131–132.
8. Vico, *Autobiography*, p. 155.

cord the maxims of the academic sages and the practices of the political sages."

By elevating philology to the rank of a science, in making it conform to philosophical principles, and by giving philosophy concretion, in making it conform to the facts, Vico devised such a system for studying the history of human nature in its development from consciousness to knowledge. For by the mutual action of philology and philosophy the facts of consciousness are found to be supported by the ideas of knowledge; authority is shown to contain reason, and reason to be implied in authority; certainty implies truth, and truth originates in certainty. Historical knowledge is therefore a knowledge of ideas, with which philosophy is concerned, and a knowledge of languages and things, i.e. facts, with which philology is concerned, united into one system. Through the knowledge of ideas Vico develops new principles of history, in its two aspects of geography and chronology, as well as of philosophy; and from these he develops the principles of universal history based on a metaphysic of the human mind. Through the knowledge of languages and things he derives new principles of poetry, and shows that poetry is the original means of human expression. By combining the knowledge of ideas with that of facts into the system of philosophy and philology Vico is thus able to construct the ideal eternal history which all the particular histories of the nations exemplify in their rise, development, *stasis*, decline and fall.[9]

## Ideas and Facts

The ideal and factual cannot be understood apart from one another. Facts alone are meaningless. Ideas without

9. Ibid., pp. 167-169.

facts are baseless. Comprehensive knowledge can only be had by the cooperation and application of the two. Under this philosophical-philological category Vico sought to discover in the facts of languages and things the ideas through which the institutions of humanity originated. It was his contention that the language of a people contains as its cause the ancient wisdom of the race which created it. And since a knowledge of history is had by a knowledge of the modifications of the mind in which institutions originated, he held that the institution of language shed the greatest light on the history of the human race. As he had shown in his sixth academic oration, languages are the most powerful means for establishing human society.[10]

Vico was directed to look for the ancient wisdom of the first peoples in their languages by the examples set by Bacon and Plato. A further incentive came from his dissatisfaction with current etymologies. He felt that lexicons and commentaries had caused Latin, the language of the people in whose history he found exemplified the history of all the nations, to degenerate. For this reason he forced himself to read the Latin authors without help, but by entering their minds.[11] The primitive wisdom of the first founders of gentile humanity was to be sought in the origins of the Latin language because the wisdom of the Italians was held to have developed earlier and to have been far richer than that of the Greeks.[12]

Vico's dissatisfaction with Plato's *Cratylus* as well as with the etymologies of the day led him, on the basis of the principle of the uniformity of human nature, to establish the principles of a universal etymology from which to

10. Ibid., p. 144.
11. Ibid., p. 134.
12. Ibid., p. 148.

derive the origins of all the languages. His added disappointment with Bacon's *De Sapientia Veterum* led him to establish the principles of poetry, and to use them to recover the principles of mythology. By means of these principles he was able to reconstruct the sources of the fables, and thus to ascertain the fabulous history of the heroic periods of all the nations.[13]

One of the foundations on which the *New Science* is built is the simple observation that words contain ideas. Since history consists of what ideas have wrought, philology as the study of words and things embraces the whole of history and is itself philosophy insofar as it studies ideas thus signified by language. Words are the key, and philology the turnkey, by which to unlock the doors to the physics, cosmography, astronomy, chronology, geography, economy, mythology, politics, morals, in short, history, of nations.

By applying his philosophical philology Vico was able to offer a solution for the problem of the origin of language in its two forms of speech and writing, and in the origin of language to discover the thought which gave rise to the institutions of the nations. Philological criticism shows that the philosophers misunderstood the causes behind the development of language, since they held writing, or letters, to have originated separately from speech, or language. Vico asserts that they should have known, from the very definitions of the words 'grammar' and 'characters,' that speech and writing originated together. For while the definition of 'grammar' is the art of speaking, since *grammata* means letters, it should have been the art of writing. 'Characters,' on the other hand, are defined as

13. Ibid., p. 153.

ideas, forms, or models, which were originally poetic, only later becoming the alphabetic characters of articulate sounds. Thus, languages originated in writing, especially since, as he contends, the first peoples were originally 'mute.' Because Vico thought he had discovered the origin of language in writing he was able to understand what his predecessors could not, that the first peoples thought in poetic characters, communicated through fables, and wrote in hieroglyphs. This solution was achieved by means of his method of uniting philosophy, in its study of ideas, with philology, in its study of one set of facts—words.[14] Since languages are the most powerful means for establishing society, a true understanding of the origin of language is the most powerful means for understanding the origins of society.

Vico chose the Latin language as his model, aside from the fact that he chose Roman history as the model of the ideal eternal history of all the nations, because he believed it to be the one ancient language which maintained its dominance throughout its evolution, and should accordingly be a prime witness to the evolution of the thought, and consequently the institutions, represented by it. The same use, he suggests, can be made of German for the same reason.[15] The origin of speech and writing, i.e., language, is thus encompassed within the ideal eternal history of the nations. Though differing as to the time and guise of different nations, the origin of language is clearly demonstrated in the causes of the Latin language. By reconstructing these causes[16] one can recreate and thereby know the causes of the institutions of all the nations.

14. Vico, *The New Science*, p. 97: 429.
15. Ibid., p. 23, Axiom XVIII: 152.
16. Ibid., p. 5: 33.

Since language contains the total stock of ideas to which a people has thus far progressed, and since language and ideas advance at the same rate,[17] it is through the development of language, and especially the Latin language, that the development of thought and of the institutions deriving from it are to be traced. And since the Latin language, or any language which qualifies, is but a model of the language spoken by the ideal eternal history traversed in time by the histories of all nations, it is through language, in this case Latin, that the ideal eternal history of all nations can be laid bare. For the universal principle of etymology in all languages, which Vico finds in the causes of the Latin language, is this: that "words are carried over from bodies and from the properties of bodies to signify the institutions of the mind and spirit."[18] A prime illustration of this principle and of the way in which Vico's philosophical philology makes use of it is afforded by the following example of the development of a word, of the thought behind it, and of the institutions signified by it. Vico contends that the origin of the language spoken by the ideal eternal history, as exemplified by Latin, was rustic. The Latin *lex*, for example, originally meant a collection of acorns, from which *ilex*, the oak, was derived. The oak, in a sense, is a collection of acorns, while acorns were originally used to collect swine together. From *lex* was also derived the word *aquilex*, meaning a collector of waters. *Lex* next came to mean a collection of vegetables. Hence the word *legumina*. Before the people had created letters for putting the laws into writing, *lex* meant a collection of citizens. Thus, the law was originally that which was enacted and sanctioned by a collection of the people. With

17. Ibid., p. 36: 234.
18. Ibid., p. 36: 237.

the development of letters came the word *legere*, reading,[19] which means collecting all the letters of which words are composed. From *legere* was derived *intelligere*, which is intelligence, the faculty by which all the elements of things are collected and formed into a perfect idea. As the order of institutions in one sense precedes the order of ideas,* which advance at the same rate as the order of words, Vico found the order of social institutions to be this: originally the forests, then the huts, the villages, the cities, and lastly the academies.[20] Thus, by tracing the development of words the order of the ideas is derived, and thereby the evolution of the institutions represented by them. This order of ideas and of things Vico holds to be essentially the same for all languages, as a consequence of which the order of the ideal eternal history of all the nations can be established.

A self-confirming philosophical philology pertaining to the ideas and facts represented by language thus discloses "the etymologies of the native languages . . . which tell us the histories of the institutions signified by the words, beginning with their original and proper meanings and pursuing the natural progress of their metaphors according to the order of ideas, on which the history of languages must proceed."[21] It is in this way that by knowing the language of a people their customs are known, by their customs their laws, and by their laws their governments, so that in knowing the ideas represented in the facts of words

19. Ibid., p. 36: 240.

*The sense is that in which by making the institutions man makes or more thoroughly humanizes himself. His humanity or his ideas in this sense are effects of the institutions, which ideas in turn represent.

20. Ibid., p. 36: 238-239.

21. Ibid., p. 64: 354.

and things the entire history of a people can be reconstructed.

### Reason and Authority

Ideas are to facts as reason is to authority. Authority contains reason, and reason is implied in authority. The first
men of the nations created their world out of the certainties of consciousness, that is, because they were incapable
of reasoning, which evolves later, they did their creating
on the basis of authority. According to the definitions of
truth and certainty, since men were originally incapable
of truth because they were incapable of reason, which is
the source and faculty of 'inner' justice, they first governed themselves by means of 'outer' justice. They established this 'outer' form of justice on the basis of the certainty of the authority of the common sense of mankind.
In failing to understand the nature of the first men the natural law theorists ascribed the 'inner' form of justice to
them, as derived from reason, while the first principles of
justice were actually founded on the certainty of authority.[22] Vico's science is not only a history of ideas, but a
philosophy and history of authority as well. It makes use
of the same criterion by means of which the first men created the institutions of the nations, the authority of the
common consciousness of the race.

Philosophy-philology, in seeking the causes of history in
the modifications of the human mind, must take into account both authority, with which the first human thinking
began, and reason, to which it gradually evolved. Human
thinking originated in the form of sensation. At this point
man was naturally inclined to see everything in terms of

22. Ibid., p. 63: 350.

body. He therefore took to be certain everything to which he could bring the authority of the senses. This stage of consciousness is almost purely subjective and accounts for the grotesque beliefs to which the early peoples ascribed. As consciousness develops reason comes into play, and the certainties of authority, which are truths under masks or partial truths since they are uninformed by a knowledge of causes, gradually become whole truths, rendered perfect by knowledge. The subjective facts or certainties of authority, with the evolution of consciousness thus become the objective ideas or truths of reason. Authority is therefore also said to be implied in reason and reason to contain authority insofar as the two are terms in the process of the evolutionary conversion of human thought from certainty to truth. The progress of the human mind is secure when the certainties of authority and the truths of reason are united. The greatest of the sciences is consequently that which unites them by means of the joint method of philosophy-philology, confirming authority with reason and reason with authority.

According to Vico this science should give a "divine pleasure" because in the divine mind, which is all reason, authority and reason are one. Human authority stems from divine authority and consists in the freedom of the will,[23] which gradually becomes rational. Divine authority is, in jurisprudence, "the authority of property ownership,"[24] since God owned all the land. Human authority consisted in guardianship during the Heroic period, and later, during human times, in "the authority of counsel."[25] As authority developed into reason Heroic au-

23. Ibid., p. 81: 388.
24. Ibid., p. 296: 944.
25. Ibid., pp. 297–298: 945–946.

thority (guardianship) became "reason of state," by which the few who were able to understand it governed the many who were not on the basis of what was necessary for their preservation. As the human times developed the "authority of counsel" was replaced by "natural reason," which Vico describes as the only kind for which the masses of humanity have any capacity since they concern themselves with the smallest details of justice only in cases in which they participate.[26]

An example of the way in which the method of philosophy-philology confirms authority by reason and grounds reason in the facts of authority is illustrated by a passage in which Vico establishes that Neptune was the last of the major divinities to be born, and that his birth coincides with the time the Heroic age began. On the authority of the philologians he states that this was when Jason first set sail for Pontus. The Heroic age came to a close when Ulysses returned to Ithaca. The authority of the philologians he confirms with the reasoning of philosophy, and further with certain philological evidence from the *Odyssey*. The philosophic reason is that the nautical arts were developed last by the nations, since their invention requires genius, which comes last. This is confirmed by the fact that Daedalus, who invented the arts of navigation, was regarded as the symbol of genius. Lucretius, for example, uses the phrase *daedala tellus* meaning 'the ingenious earth.' On the authority of Homer Ulysses' landings are always depicted as beginning with a search for signs of habitation. Plato cites the reason for this in the fact that the first nations were afraid of the sea for a long time. This is more fully explained by Thucydides' statement that

26. Ibid., pp. 299–301: 947–951.

because of pirate raids the Greeks hesitated to live along the coasts. For these reasons Neptune always appears bearing the trident, with which he was held both by Homer and later by Plato to shake the earth. The trident, Vico explains, is the combination form of the word for 'tooth' and the prefix 'three,' which signifies the superlative; it was therefore a great hook or tooth used for grappling ships. From this Vico contends that the Greeks were afraid of the sea, i.e., Neptune, from the time Jason left until Ulysses returned home, proving its mastery and closing the Heroic age.[27] Thus, in this matter of setting the date of Neptune's birth the authority of the historians is confirmed by a philosophic reason, which in turn is confirmed by the ideas behind the etymology of the word *Daedalus*. These are then confirmed by the further authority of Homer, who is confirmed by Plato, who is confirmed by Thucydides, all of whom are confirmed by a reasoned account of the word 'trident,' which is again confirmed by the authority of Homer and Plato. "Philological proofs enable us to see in fact the institutions we have meditated in idea as touching this world of nations, in accordance with Bacon's method of philosophizing, which is 'think (and) see' . . . (*cogitare videre*) . . . With the help of . . . philosophical proofs, . . . philological proofs both confirm their own authority by reason and at the same time confirm reason by their authority."[28]

## Truth and Certainty

As ideas are to facts and reason is to authority so truth is to certainty. Authority pertains to facts, from which is de-

27. Ibid., pp. 192–193: 634.
28. Ibid., p. 65: 359.

rived a consciousness of what is certain in human affairs. Reason concerns ideas, from which is derived a knowledge of the true. As the sphere of consciousness widens with the development of human reason, so authority becomes rational, and what were certainties are perfected and converted into truths. Certainties are would-be truths which, since reason is undeveloped, are incapable of complete realization. They are, as it were, potential truths, whose actuality is dependent on the capacity of reason to fully develop itself. According to Vico human nature consists of body, mind, and speech, which is midway between the two. Concerning justice, as cited under the category of authority, the laws were originally certainties expressed in the ages before speech was invented in terms of the body. When the art of speaking evolved from the art of writing, ideas as to what was just in the laws became articulated in the certitudes of spoken formulas. Then with the advance of human nature from body through speech to mind, with the unfolding of reason, these certitudes, which depended on the facts, became truths in the ideas of justice themselves.[29]

The formal antithesis between certainty and truth can be demonstrated, for example, by Vico's consideration of the history of jurisprudence, which shows a development from what is certain in the laws to what is true. Aside from divine legal judgments, to which people first had recourse, at first ordinary and then extraordinary human judgments developed from the divine. The first type of legal judgment consisted of "extreme verbal scrupulousness," as characterized by such expressions as *qui cadit virgula, caussa cadit*: 'He who drops a comma loses his

29. Ibid., p. 347: 1045.

case,' or *uti lingua nuncupassit, ita ius esto*: 'as the tongue
has declared, so shall it be binding.' The idea of justice
indicated by such expressions is that right is uniformly
based on the strict observance of certain verbal formulas.[30]
Since these had originated in divine judgments, they carried with them the sanction of the gods. Thus in the first
human times the beginnings of justice were based on the
certainty of authority as instituted by divine providence.
For in order for the nations to preserve themselves, since
they were incapable of governing themselves by means of
truth and natural equity, providence ordained that they
should be governed by certainty and civil equity, which
consists in adherence to the letter of the law regardless of
the different natures of the cases.[31]

With the full development of human reason the certainties of consciousness become translated into the truths of
knowledge, and human legal judgments, previously called
"ordinary," are now referred to as "extraordinary."[32] The
idea of justice is no longer that of finding certainty in the
strict adherence to verbal formulas, but of finding truth
in the rational contemplation of the facts of each individual case. And as certainty is, as it were, truth uninformed
by a knowledge of causes, so the truth in the laws considers the specific causes determining acts.

The evolution of law, or of the idea of justice, is an
instance which confirms the general evolution of the human mind from certainty to truth and from authority to
reason. In the divine mind truth and justice and truth and
certainty are one. The human mind in finding justice in
truth in the example of law, and in uniting the true with

30. Ibid., pp. 304, 309, 311: 955, 965, 968.
31. Ibid., p. 51: 328.
32. Ibid., p. 313: 974.

the certain of the facts in general, is comparable to the divine.

The idea of law, of language, of poetics or politics, is the idea of the universal and eternal development of these facts or institutions of the nations from their origin in the certain to their end in the true. Turned about, the true allows us to consider "this world of nations in its eternal idea, by that property of every science, noted by Aristotle, that science has to do with what is universal and eternal (*scientia debet esse de universalibus et aeternis*)," while the certain permits us "to see in fact this world of nations which we have studied in idea, following the method of philosophizing that Francis Bacon, Lord of Verulam, did most to render certain, but carrying it over from the things of nature, on which he composed his book *Cogitata (et) visa*, to the civil institutions of mankind."[33]

*Knowledge and Consciousness*

Ideas and facts, reason and authority, truth and certainty, are the three aspects of the general method called philosophy-philology. In a sense this method is derived from the genetic principle that theories must begin where their subject matters begin. Thus, history, which is essentially the history of mind, must begin where mind begins, at the dawn of consciousness, and trace its development until it reaches knowledge. History is therefore a composite of the facts, authority, and certainties of consciousness and the ideas, reason, and truths of knowledge. The method of history is, accordingly, a method which combines and unites into one system these philologic certainties and their concomitant philosophic or eternal truths. Philosophy demonstrates the eternal truths of the causes

33. Ibid., p. 26: 163.

of history; philology reconstructs the certainties of their effects.

The following example illustrates the general method of philosophy-philology concerning, in this case, the origin of poetic astronomy. In order to discover its origin Vico combines three facts of philology with two philosophic truths. The first fact established by philology is that astronomy was developed by the Chaldeans; the second, that the Egyptians became acquainted with the quadrant and knew about the elevation of the pole through the Phoenicians, who learned it from the Chaldeans; the third, that the Phoenicians taught astral theology to the Greeks. From philosophy Vico derives these truths: first, that in the early stages of the development of nations, since religious liberty is not practiced, the people do not readily admit foreign deities; second, that an optical illusion causes the planets to appear larger than the fixed stars.

Having premised these two philosophic truths Vico then proceeds to determine the validity of the facts established by philology. On the principle that the planets appear larger than the fixed stars he finds that all the nations, since all look to the heavens, uniformly assigned the gods to the planets and the heroes to the stars. When the Phoenicians appeared among the Egyptians and later among the Greeks, as when the Greeks met the Latins, on the principle that early peoples do not readily admit foreign deities, they found the gods and heroes already established in their orbits. Hence, poetic astronomy originated not in Chaldea but in the common consciousness of the race, its certainties remaining until learned astronomy gave them true expression.[34] In this way Vico shows how philol-

34. Ibid., pp. 227–228: 727–728.

ogy, in its study of facts, authority, and certainty, in part confirms or denies, or is confirmed or denied by, philosophy in its study of ideas, reason, and truth.

The history of humanity is the history of its unfolding. It neither began with knowledge nor ended in consciousness. Human nature, unfulfilled by the facts and certainties of authority, progressed to the ideas and truths of reason. To study the ideas and truths of knowledge in a vacuum, as the rationalists did, was to ignore the development of man, and also to deny the possibility of his future development. To combine this study with the facts and certainties of consciousness is to admit the progress of man and society, and to leave the way open for its continuing. The rationalists' reliance on their own logical intellect leads to the conceit that the history of humanity ends with them. Furthermore, it places their individual consciousness above the common consciousness of the race. But for Vico the common consciousness, if only by virtue of its being held in common, is that much greater than the individual consciousness. It is in fact the ultimate authority, in which all particular facts, certitudes, and authorities find assurance and in which, by the way, all the prejudices and abstractions of the philosophers are levelled. It is the embodiment of the popular or poetic wisdom of the race, which gradually becomes converted to the esoteric wisdom of the philosophers. This vulgar wisdom, imaginative, intuitive, concrete, contingent, probable, non-logical, prephilosophical, is as necessary, indeed more necessary, to a complete understanding of human development as is reason. For Descartes the imagination stood in the way of knowledge.[35] For Vico it is indispensably on the way. *Verum*

35. Vico, *Autobiography*, p. 30.

and *factum* are convertible because over the long process of history certainty, authority, and consciousness have actually been converted into truth, reason, and knowledge. The method for understanding this conversion and for making it is the concomitant method of philology, in its study of the facts of "religions, languages, laws, customs, property rights, conveyances, sovereign powers, governments, classes . . . arms, trials, penalties, wars, peaces, and alliances,"[36] and philosophy, whose study is the ideas these represent.

As history is the story of reason becoming aware of itself, so the method of history is designed to ascertain and reconstruct the process by which reason has developed. The history of humanity is therefore to be discovered by means of a philology considered philosophically in idea, and a philosophy philologically grounded in fact. Philology, which has as its objects languages and things, approaches history in terms of the effects to which ideas have given rise, while philosophy, which has ideas as its objects, approaches history on the side of the causes from which the facts have originated. Philology thus confirms philosophy and is confirmed by it. History is essentially philosophy, insofar as it is the study of the ideas that have formed society. But it is also philology, insofar as it is the study of the institutions caused by these ideas.

36. Ibid., pp. 157, 171.

# 6

# The Method of Knowledge:
# The Art of
# Historical Criticism

The theory of the criterion of knowledge with which Vico began to construct the *New Science Concerning the Common Nature of the Nations* became extended under his hand to include a method of knowledge which would satisfy this criterion, and which consisted, in its primary aspect, of constructing out of the modifications of the human mind, the causes of the world of nations; and in its secondary aspect, of confirming the truth of the causes of history, i.e., philosophy, with the certainty of their effects, i.e., philology. In its third principal aspect the method of knowledge is the art of criticism, which serves to complement the construction of the other two. In the history of human development, Vico found, the Art of Criticism is preceded by the Art of Topics. In the same way, poetry precedes philosophy by about 2000 years, and imagination intellect. Topics is the art of apprehending, acquiring,[1] or inventing what is necessary and useful for the business of life, while criticism is the art of judging. Man first apprehends particulars, then judges, and finally looks for uni-

1. Flint, p. 132.

versals.[2] As the historian cannot rely on intellect to the exclusion of imagination, so he cannot rely on criticism to the exclusion of topics.[3] Criticism and Topics must be conjoined in the mind of the historian as knowing and making are, as the ideas of philosophy are conjoined with the facts of philology. History must be acquired, apprehended, or created; verified,[4] comprehended, and known. In short, it must be critically reconstructed from the data in which it is given, "sifting" and recreating "the truth as to the founders of the (gentile) nations from the popular traditions of the nations they founded."[5] What Vico calls the metaphysical art of criticism is actually the joint method of philosophy-philology critically employed, that is, it is the method of philosophical-philological criticism, which reinforces the method of philosophical-philological construction. These three thus delineated aspects of the method of knowledge do not occur separately or in any order however, but are conjoined in the mind of the historian and applied as one method, from which is derived a true knowledge of the history of humanity.

The art of criticism is specifically employed to discover the times and places in which the ideas giving rise to the institutions of the nations originated, and also to discover the identity of the founders of the nations. The criterion Vico's criticism uses is the common consciousness of the race, which providence instituted among all the nations and on the basis of which they constructed their world. The critical aspect of the New Science thus combines the truths of philosophy with the certainties of

2. Vico, Autobiography, pp. 123, 124.
3. Flint, p. 133.
4. Ibid., p. 61.
5. Vico, Autobiography, p. 167.

philology in relation to a chronology and geography of the institutions established by providence through human consciousness. Since the course the nations follow has been ordered by providence, the demonstrations of this aspect of the *Science* are likewise guaranteed.[6]

The master key of Vico's method of knowledge in general, and of its critical aspect in particular, lay in the discovery that the first people of the world were poets, who thought in poetic characters; that in their poetry, languages, laws, customs, fables, and mythologies are to be found the common wisdom of the human race, which is different in form but the same in content as the esoteric wisdom of the philosophers. The discovery that imaginative universals, in which the first peoples thought, are rudimentary forms of intelligible universals, led Vico to adopt this philosophical-philological method of criticism by which he neither accepted the traditions of the nations at face value nor rejected them as 'Plato's noble lies;' instead he interpreted them according to the way he reasoned they were first conceived. Thus he interprets the epics of Homer as "civil histories of ancient Greek customs." These can then be shown to be two great repositories of the natural law of the Greek peoples.[7]

Through the principle of imaginative universals or poetic characters, in which terms the first people did their creating, Vico is able to critically interpret the myths and fables ascribing the founding of states to sages or law-givers, and the accomplishment of great feats to certain heroes or champions. He shows that because the vulgar had a *genius* or talent for creating poetic characters, the wisdom ascribed to the founders of nations is nothing less than the

6. Vico, *The New Science*, p. 62: 348.
7. Ibid., p. 23, Axiom XX: 156.

common sense of the race personified in an individual man. By the same token the heroes which the fables abound in are but poetic characters or universals in whom the deeds of a hundred ordinary men are epitomized. It is in this sense that the first people of the human race were true poets: they were themselves the founders of the nations. And Homer is none other than a poetic character himself created by the Greek people.[8]

On the basis of the discovery of the true character of the first human thinking, Vico is able to arrive at various truths concerning the history of remote antiquity. These truths had been obscured because of certain fallacious tendencies on the parts of the philosophers and philologians and also the ancient peoples themselves. The first axiom with which Vico begins the *New Science* explores these tendencies with the purpose of laying down the rules of historical criticism. 1. He asserts that because the human mind is uncertain, whenever it is ignorant of the true nature of things it measures them by itself, and that one of the mind's properties is to magnify anything of which it is ignorant, *omne ignotum pro magnifico est.*[9] Ignorance on the part of the philosophers and philologians is the source of that fallacy which Vico calls 'magnificent opinions,' whereby the scholars interpreted the history of the early nations as either all dark and without light in comparison to their own, or as enlightened as their own. 2. Another property of the mind causes men ignorant of the past to judge it by the present.[10] With this axiom Vico sets forth the fallacious methods by which the philosophers and philologians imposed their own ideas on the history

8. Ibid., p. 269: 873.
9. Ibid., p. 18, Axiom I: 120, 121.
10. Ibid., Axiom II: 122.

of humanity. These he labels the 'conceit of nations' and the 'conceit of scholars.' 3. The conceit of nations has every nation believing it created the comforts of life before any other and tracing its history back to the origin of the world.[11] Due to this conceit the so-called evidence of tradition, which has been carried over in the fables and myths, and the so-called authority of the philologians who proceeded on the basis of this evidence, cannot be regarded as trustworthy. 4. Like the conceit of nations that of scholars consists in the belief that their knowledge is as ancient as the world. On the basis of this axiom Vico holds that all the notions of the scholars venerating the wisdom of the first men are likewise untrustworthy.[12] For these reasons the principles of historical development could neither be derived from the philosophers nor the philologians but, as Vico says, "we must reckon as if there were no books in the world"[13] and create them for ourselves.

The theory of knowledge and the method of introspection combined with the philosophical-philological reconstruction of ideas and facts is the equivalent of proceeding 'as if there were no books in the world.' And the metaphysical art of criticism is coincident with it, for it frees the method of historical knowledge from exclusive bondage to authority, instead emphasizing a critical analysis of the facts in the light of the ideas which give them meaning. The meaning of the fables and myths has been lost over the years as they passed through the conceits of philosophers and philologians. Their original meanings can be recovered by means of the art of criticism, which

11. Ibid., p. 19, Axiom III: 125.
12. Ibid., Axiom IV: 127, 128.
13. Ibid., p. 52: 330.

casts off the embellishments of nations and of scholars and exhumes the truth from the ideas which the naked facts then truly represent.

An example of the way in which the art of criticism shows up the magnificent opinions of the scholars is the following. According to previous axioms, and to principles of Heroic politics, Vico asserts that the philologians' rendering of the words 'people,' 'king,' 'liberty,' led the philosophers to misconstrue the age of Heroism. Under 'people' they thought the Heroic people included the plebeians; by 'king' they understood a 'monarch,' and 'liberty' they interpreted as popular liberty. Moreover, their conceit caused them to apply to the Heroic age a rational form of justice, a notion that glory is gained by benevolence, and a desire for immortality, all of which they themselves possessed. But Achilles, an exemplary hero, was hardly *just* in vowing to let his dogs eat Hector's body, rather unconcerned with *glory*, having deserted the Greeks, and not at all *desirous of immortality* in preferring to be the lowliest slave alive rather than remain in the netherworld. Furthermore, since the heroes swore eternal enmity against the plebeians, the term *people* could not have applied to the latter, but only to the patricians, who alone enjoyed liberty. This so-called *popular liberty* was maintained if not on the physical then on the economic enslavement of the plebeians. Finally, the *kings* were not the *monarchs* of later times, but a handful of aristocrats, who as the fittest survived by enslaving and afflicting the plebians under their rule. By following their conceit to the end of its tether, however, the philosophers concluded that the monarchs, according to their sense of justice, and in their desire for glory and immortality, consecrated themselves, their families, and their entire estates to the poor.[14] By a philological criticism of the words 'people,' 'king,' 'liberty,' confirmed by a philosophical criticism of the ideas behind the customs of the early peoples, including further evidence from the Homeric poems, Vico holds the conclusion of the scholars to be, not only erroneous, but absurd. For this reason he says of the four previous axioms, the source of all the fallacies concerning the origin of nations, that they "give us the basis for refuting all opinions hitherto held about the principles of humanity. The refutations turn on the improbabilities, absurdities, contradictions, and impossibilities of these opinions."[15]

The art of criticism proceeds not only by casting off the errors with which tradition has become bound, but also by turning them to good use. One case is Vico's account of the transfer of the names Hercules and Evander from Greece to Latium in accordance with the conceit of nations. Greek tradition had it that the actual Hercules and Evander had taken up residence in Latium during the latter's barbaric beginnings. But in their beginnings early peoples refuse to admit foreign deities and customs to their lands and jealously repel outside influence. With the advance of civilization, however, they eagerly do the opposite. On the principle of the conceit of nations in attaching themselves to an illustrious heritage it was therefore much later and of their own accord that the civilized Latins renounced their true founder, Fidius, for Hercules, the founder of the Greeks, substituting the oath *mehercule, edepol, mecastor* for their original oath *medius fidius*. For the same reasons it was then that they disavowed

14. Ibid., pp. 201, 202, 203, 206: 666–669.
15. Ibid., p. 25: 163.

their own poets in favor of the Greek, Evander.[16] Reconstructing the way in which these particular Greek figures became Latinized is an instance of transforming a misleading account into an accurate one. It is an example of the art of criticism which, as an aspect of the general method of knowledge, likewise focuses its attention on the causes of history, the modifications of the mind.

History, as conceived by Vico, is the study of the progressive development of the human mind. Criticism, no less than the study of ideas and facts, reason and authority, truth and certainty, i.e., philosophy-philology, and the method of introspection, serve and complete the function of historical knowledge. From the point of view of criticism, tradition as it is passed on in fable and mythology, poetry, laws, and customs, contains truth, though the original meaning of tradition is hidden. To be known it must be reinterpreted by a critical-constructive method for discovering and demonstrating the modifications of the mind out of which it was first created.

16. Ibid., pp. 238–239: 765–766.

# 7

# The Purpose of Knowledge

A theory of knowledge would be incomplete, not to say meaningless, if it did not define the purpose which knowledge should fulfill. Vico's predecessors regarded the purpose of historical knowledge as didactic, a matter of setting down precepts or examples for the teaching of prudence.[1] For Vico, knowledge and prudence had to be distinct.[2] Although Hobbes had shown the demonstrability of history, he later held that anything based on historical knowledge was too dubious to be of much value[3] even as precept or example. The success of physics also contributed to derogating what was thought to be the purpose of a knowledge of history.[4] With a wave of his hand Descartes dealt the final blow to history, dismissing it altogether on the grounds that anything that has developed gradually is necessarily imperfect.[5] But this includes not only history, in its ordinary meaning, but human nature and the

1. Vico, *Autobiography*, p. 23.
2. Flint, p. 62.
3. Vico, *Autobiography*, p. 28.
4. Ibid., p. 26.
5. Ibid., p. 29.

human mind itself. According to Vico the true sphere of knowledge is limited to history, to that area in which the human mind is truly creative. Yet history and historical knowledge are themselves unlimited. History is universal. It comprises all the human mind has achieved in all the nations of the world, from its birth to its present development; all the arts and sciences, politics and religions of humanity. A knowledge of history is therefore a complete understanding of everything the human mind has undertaken to fashion in the civil world. It is due to this concept of history that Vico calls his work a *new* science of humanity, for it contained "a theme both new and grand, to unite in one principle all knowledge human and divine."[6] Comprehensiveness is part of Vico's criterion of knowledge. In order for knowledge to be true it must be total. Not only is true knowledge limited to history then, but total knowledge is history.

History itself has no purpose. Like the process of life, the process of history is an end in itself. Like life too, the only purpose it can be said to have is to continue. Knowledge, on the other hand, has a purpose. As history is the study of the evolution of the human mind, so the purpose of knowledge, in seeking to understand what the human mind has achieved in the past, is to understand what the human mind is capable of achieving in the present and future. Man is a historical being. By knowing himself he can know the history of the world that has gone before him; yet he seeks to know the history of the world in order that he may know himself. Since the world has been created out of the modifications of our own human mind, by knowing the modifications of our mind we know

6. Ibid., p. 146.

the world, and it is by knowing the modifications of the mind and thus the world that we know ourselves. Even in his time Vico recognized "that the knowledge of oneself is for each of us the greatest incentive to the compendious study of every branch of learning."[7] It was his contention that the only reason anyone desires to know anything is that he may better know himself. On the other hand, the only reason anyone fails to know anything is because he does not wish to.[8] It is in man's power, indeed it is in man's nature, to know. The man who does not seek knowledge, or who fails to attain it, "is guilty of treason"[9] against himself. History, in the largest sense, is the study of oneself. It is therefore admirably suited to fulfill the purpose of knowledge.

But the purpose of knowledge is not only to 'know thyself,' but that in knowing oneself one may so act as to benefit oneself and humanity at large. The purpose of knowledge is not to become draped in fine logic or bedizened with learning, but to do or make.[10] The final goal of knowledge is action. For "man, in his proper being as man, consists of mind and spirit, or, if we prefer, of intellect and will. It is the function of wisdom to fulfill both these parts in man, the second by way of the first, to the end that by a mind illuminated by knowledge of the highest institutions, the spirit may be led to choose the best."[11]

The *New Science* is, among everything else, a demonstration of Vico's theory of knowledge. It demonstrates the

7. Ibid., p. 140.
8. Ibid.
9. Ibid., p. 141.
10. Flint, p. 133.
11. Vico, *The New Science*, p. 70: 364.

possibility and criterion, the methods and purpose of knowledge. It also demonstrates the truth of the saying, misquoted by Vico—*Pusilla res hic mundus est, nisi id, quod quaerit, omnis mundus habeat*—that "this world is a paltry thing unless all the world may find (therein) what it seeks."[12] For the truth is that the world is as vast as the mind that thinks it, and the mind is as vast as the world it thinks.

12. Ibid., p. 373: 1096.

# Afterword

Vico regarded the *New Science* as the culmination of his life's work and the testament to its value. It is. But no more than his own life is a testament to his work. The principles he found operating in humanity's ascent to knowledge he also saw at work in his own history. As the *New Science* is a demonstration of the theory of knowledge, so his own life also demonstrates that theory: in his development of knowledge can be found an exemplification of the intellectual evolution of the race from the apprehension of fact to the contemplation of idea, from the certainty of authority to the truth of reason, in short from consciousness to knowledge. In a greater sense than the phrase can be applied to most men, Vico created himself, and then turned around and narrated the story of his creation in the perfected form which knowledge brings to consciousness.

Vico created himself in that he was essentially self-taught. He was, as a friend referred to him, an "autodidact."[1] Although he attended lectures and studied under

1. Vico, *Autobiography*, p. 136.

one teacher or another, he found them all wanting and
acted on the partial realization that he would do better to
look for truth in his own mind rather than in the lecture
halls or classes of the great. He applied himself directly,
instead of through others, to the subjects that interested
him. Without the authority of a teacher or school to re-
vert to, he was forced to rely almost exclusively on his own
reason.[2] "Vico blessed his good fortune in having no teacher
whose words he had sworn by, and he felt most grateful
for those woods in which, guided by his good genius, he
had followed the main course of his studies untroubled
by sectarian prejudice; for in the city taste in letters
changed every two or three years like styles in dress."[3]

This good fortune he later concluded was nothing less
than providential. In fact, his life as he describes it is
in one respect a demonstration of providence. The first
*New Science*, which was expounded negatively, consisted
of two volumes. Vico had lost his sponsor and could not
afford to bring out the work himself. He discovered that
by using a positive method of exposition what the work
would lose in volume it would gain in quality, and that
he would be able to subsidize it. This was just one more in-
dication of the offices of providence turning apparent
evils into goods. In whatever adversity he suffered, whether
losing a competition for a chair at the university, receiving unfavorable reviews for his publications, or having to
publish his work at his own expense, he saw the work-
ings of providence.

The same creative reason Vico applied to his own development, which he later found developing in the race,
stood him in good stead when he came to consider the his-

2. Flint, pp. 63–64.
3. Vico, *Autobiography*, p. 133.

tory of humanity. As early as 1708, 36 years before the third edition of the *New Science*, he shows himself in the academic oration[4] of that date to have severed all ties with authority and to have reached that pinnacle where creative reason alone is sufficient to disclose the principles operating in human evolution. By reconstructing history, by applying his creative reason to the facts of mankind, Vico came to realize that he was making these facts his own,[5] and that this was both possible and justifiable because they were his own. He could more readily do this because what he discovered in the mental development of the race as the gradual progress from imagination to intellect had been synthesized in himself. His creative reason was a well-balanced composite of imagination and intellect, of poetic and philosophic wisdom. His own development was from imagination to intellect, or poetry to philosophy, never however losing the brightness of the imaginative faculty in the intellectual bogs of philosophy. It was his imaginative or poetic faculty, so indispensable to the historian, which allowed him to enter the minds of the first men, recreate and understand their history. "Vico must have lived intensely in his primeval forest and its clearings, his theories as to what happened there are so distinct and elaborate."[6] It was his understanding of the need for imagination that led him to call eloquence, the expression of poetry as opposed to prose, of vulgar or poetic as opposed to philosophic wisdom, "nothing but wisdom speaking."[7] In one of his academic orations Vico made "a digression in a style half way between that of poetry and

4. Flint, pp. 58–59.
5. Croce, p. 23.
6. Adams, p. 187.
7. Vico, *Autobiography*, p. 199.

that of prose." He says of this that "such indeed should be the historical style, in the opinion of Cicero . . . For history should use, (Cicero) says, 'words for the most part taken from the poets'; perhaps because the historians were still clinging to their ancient possession, for, as is clearly demonstrated in the *New Science*, the first historians of the nations were the poets."[8]

Vico's life illustrates the development and synthesis of imagination and intellect no less than the development and synthesis of the factual and the ideal or, in general, philology-philosophy. Vico was a student of poetry and also wrote poetry. He was a legal theorist as well as a practitioner of law. Early in his study of law "he began to realize how the legal discipline is less than half learned by the method of study which is commonly observed."[9] He saw, for example, how the jurisconsults paid the greatest attention to the wording of the laws, but that it was the medieval interpreters who extrapolated general principles of justice and were themselves the true philosophers of natural equity.[10] This disclosure of the strictness with which the jurisconsults observed the letter of the law prepared the way he was to travel in his study of the ideas embodied in the Latin language. Much later, for example, during one of his academic orations, he was able to demonstrate how "from the interpretation of the words he elicited the sense" of a particular legal definition.[11] His discovery of the medievalists' abstractions was to lead to his inquiry into the very principles of universal justice.[12]

8. Ibid., p. 180.
9. Ibid., p. 121.
10. Ibid., p. 116.
11. Ibid., p. 162.
12. Ibid., p. 116.

What he later found was that justice came from God, but that the facts of civil law gradually approximated ideal law,[13] and that human reason enlarged and perfected the laws granted on authority. This pattern Vico eventually realized was not limited only to the sphere of law: the entire moral realm progressed from the factual to the ideal, from authority to reason, from certainty to truth, and from consciousness to knowledge. At this point his theory of knowledge was unfolding and a *New Science*, a body of "comprehensive knowledge coherent in all its parts,"[14] was being created.

The unity of human knowledge had always been Vico's undiscerned aim. He had said that his chair at the university "was the one that should give direction to minds and make them universal; that others were concerned with the various parts of knowledge, but his should teach it as an integral whole in which each part accords with every other and gets its meaning from the whole."[15] His writings are themselves all of a piece, culminating in the *New Science*. He had written *On the Ancient Wisdom of the Italians, On the Method of the Studies of Our Time,* which was augmented by *On the One Principle of Universal Law.* From the latter followed *On the Consistency of Philosophy* and *On the Consistency of Philology,* in which "he begins to reduce philology to scientific principles,"[16] thus leading to the first, second, and third *New Science*. Before this time, between 1699 and 1708, his academic orations had all sown the seeds that were to germinate into these and the final work. They do not deal with dif-

13. Flint, p. 45.
14. Vico, *Autobiography*, p. 117.
15. Ibid., p. 199.
16. Ibid., p. 158.

ferent subjects as much as with different aspects of the
same subject. Vico did not "so much pass from one piece
of work to another, as from the expression or exposition
of one stage of his own life to that of another. It was an essentially self-developing, self-forming genius, which stead-
ily laboured from internal, inborn impulse, to reduce
everything that came within its range of apprehension to
unity and harmony and conformity with its own ideals."[17]
This unity eventually took shape in the synthesis of all that
is encompassed in the philosophical and philological
realms of knowledge.

It was only later in his development that Vico's *ideals*
made themselves known however. His incipient studies
in poetry, language, rhetoric, and law only led him in the
direction his mental life was to take. Vico's own evolution, in microcosm, exemplifies the general evolution and
synthesis he found operating in the human race: the evolution from consciousness to knowledge. From his study of
laws he went past the ideas behind the laws until "there
began to dawn on him, without his being aware of it, the
thought of meditating an ideal eternal law that should be
observed in a universal city after the idea or design of
providence, upon which idea have since been founded all
the commonwealths of all times and all nations."[18]

As the *New Science* is a demonstration of Vico's theory
of knowledge applied to the life of the race, so in the *Autobiography* he applies his theory of knowledge to the life
of the individual, himself. He was insistent to note, however, that knowledge is not the property of the individual
consciousness, but only of the common consciousness of
the race; although it may seem he found the principles of

17. Flint, p. 40.
18. Vico, *Autobiography*, p. 122.

mental development in his own mind, as he accused Descartes of doing, and then applied them to the race, it was actually the reverse, except as he looked through his own mind in its role as a usable product of history. Self-knowledge is in any case impossible without knowledge of the larger self, in which the individual self is in both senses comprehended.

Vico not only regarded Descartes' reliance on the individual consciousness as delusive, but he regarded his autobiographical material, a result of this reliance, as a total fraud. He considered Descartes' description of his studies impossible, and due to his failure to grasp, to his complete disavowal of, historical method. "We shall not here feign what René Descartes craftily feigned as to the method of his studies simply in order to exalt his own philosophy and mathematics and degrade all the other studies included in divine and human erudition. Rather, with the candor proper to a historian, we shall narrate plainly and step by step the entire series of Vico's studies, in order that the proper and natural causes of his particular development as a man of letters may be known."[19]

Vico was so imbued with his theory of knowledge and with the concept of historical development that he could not have done otherwise than to trace his own intellectual evolution in accordance with the principles he discovered in and for the evolution of humanity. By tracing the effects of each stage of his mind's development he was able to grasp their causes, to recreate and thereby know, through the modifications of his mind, the process of his own history. "As may be seen, he wrote (his *Autobiography*) as a philosopher, meditating the causes, nat-

19. Ibid., p. 113.

ural and moral, and the occasions of fortune; why even
from childhood he had felt an inclination for certain studies and an aversion from others; what opportunities and
obstacles had advanced or retarded his progress; and
lastly the effect of his own exertions in right directions,
which were destined later to bear fruit in those reflections
on which he built his final work, the *New Science*, which
was to demonstrate that his intellectual life was bound
to have been such as it was and not otherwise."[20]

20. Ibid., p. 182.

# Bibliography

## PRIMARY SOURCES

1. Vico, Giambattista, *Autobiography*, tr. by Max Harold Fisch & Thomas Goddard Bergin, Cornell University Press, New York, 1944.

2. ___, *The New Science*, tr. by Max Harold Fisch & Thomas Goddard Bergin, Cornell University Press, New York, 1968.

## SECONDARY SOURCES

1. Adams, H. P., *The Life and Writings of Giambattista Vico*, George Allen & Unwin Ltd., London, 1935.

2. Berry, Thomas, *The Historical Theory of Giambattista Vico*, The Catholic University of America Press, Washington, 1949.

3. Child, Arthur, *Making and Knowing in Hobbes, Vico, and Dewey*, University of California Publications in Philosophy, Berkeley, 16 (1953).

4. Collingwood, R. G., *The Idea of History*, Clarendon Press, Oxford, 1946.

5. Croce, Benedetto, *Aesthetic*, tr. by D. Ainsle, Macmillan & Co. Ltd., London, 1922.

6. ___, *The Philosophy of Giambattista Vico*, tr. by R. G. Collingwood, Macmillan, N.Y., 1913.

7. Fisch, M. H., "Vico on Roman Law," *Essays in Political Theory Presented to G. H. Sabine*, Konvitz & Murphy, Ithaca, 1948.

8. Flint, Robert, *Vico*, Wm. Blackwood & Sons, Edinburgh, 1884.

9. Lowith, Karl, *Meaning in History*, University of Chicago Press, Chicago, 1949.

10. Vaughan, C. E., *Studies in the History of Political Philosophy, Before and After Rousseau*, Vol. 1, Manchester University Press, Manchester, 1925.